Faithful unto Death

MARCIA BENDER

© 2024 by CAM Books, a wholly owned, for-profit subsidiary of Christian Aid Ministries, Berlin, Ohio.

All rights reserved. No part of this book may be reproduced or stored in any retrieval system, in any form or by any means, electronic or mechanical, without written permission from the publisher except for brief quotations embodied in critical articles and reviews.

ISBN: 978-1-63813-390-2

Cover and interior design: Kristi Yoder

Cover and interior artwork by Lydia Bauman

Printed in the USA

Published by:

CAM Books
P.O. Box 355
Berlin, Ohio 44610 USA
Phone: 330.893.4828
Fax: 330.893.4893
cambooks.org

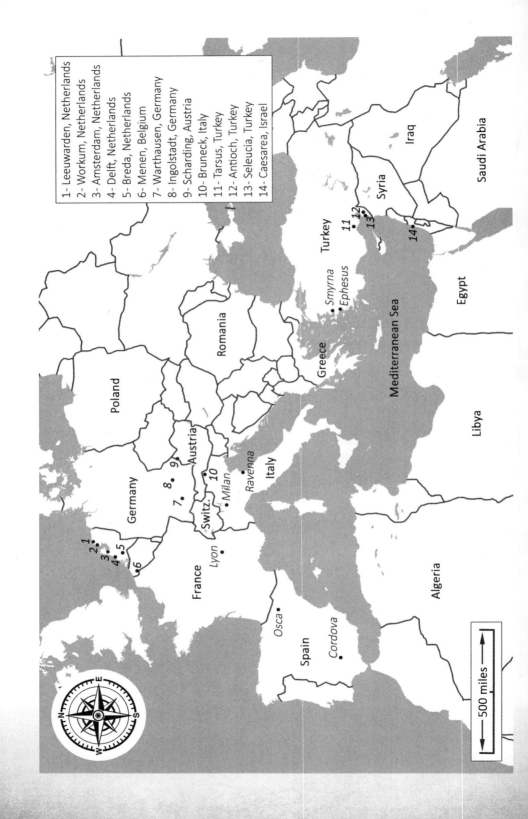

Contents

Introduction 7
1. "There Has to Be Something Better" 9
2. "I Have Served My Lord Eighty-Six Years" 19
3. "I Am a Christian" 29
4. "Bury Me With the Fetters" 39
5. "I Feel No Pain" 47
6. "I Shall Never Deny the Only True God" 55
7. "I Am Not So Timid" 65

8.	"I Will Never Again Give Up My Faith"	73
9.	"We Worship the True God"	81
10.	"I Will Remain a Christian"	89
11.	"If You Can Burn This Flower"	99
12.	"Watch the Smoke"	105
13.	"My Happiness Comes From God"	113
14.	"My Shirt Collar... A Sign"	121
15.	"Why Have You Betrayed Me?"	129
16.	"My Blood Will Be Seen in the Sun"	137
17.	"I Never Slept Better"	143
18.	"I Have Nothing Else"	153
19.	"I Would Rather Die"	161
20.	"Here Comes the Wolf"	169
	Conclusion	177
	About the Author	183

Introduction

Persecution of God's people has been common throughout history. Thousands—no, millions—of people have given their lives for their faith. If there is one word that describes these martyrs, it is *FAITHFUL*.

Formidable. Is that what comes to your mind at the thought of reading the *Martyrs Mirror?* Indeed, the *Martyrs Mirror* is formidable! The size of the book can discourage us from reading it, as can the old-fashioned writing style. But as we read it, the contents will inspire awe at the faithfulness of the people we meet in its pages.

As I spent hours mining the expanse of the *Martyrs Mirror,* I was awestruck by the indomitable faith of the thousands of people who suffered tortures and atrocities that are beyond human comprehension.

We cannot begin to imagine, even when we read these horrors, what these people suffered because of their faith in God.

In these stories, you will find men and women who were "faithful unto death." These men and women, some of them mere youths, laid down their lives because they believed God and His Word. They esteemed "the reproach of Christ" greater riches than the treasures of this world.

Throughout these accounts, I have endeavored to portray the main details as accurately as possible when they are given in the *Martyrs Mirror*. But as is true in a lot of historical writing, there are many things that are unknown.

Hence the use of imagination, based on other accounts and writings of life in that era. It is not my intent to mislead anyone as to the facts of the story. The use of imagination was sometimes needed to tie the different parts of a story together.

For the most accurate reading of an account, readers are encouraged to go to the *Martyrs Mirror* itself. Page numbers to the corresponding account in the *Martyrs Mirror* are included at the beginning of each chapter.

Use of explanatory footnotes is intended to help the reader better understand the stories. They are often used to clarify when a story contains more fiction than most.

Let these stories inspire you to be the person God wants you to be. And I trust your appetite will be whetted enough to pick up that "formidable" book and read it for yourself. There are many, many martyrs whose accounts I have not touched.

As you read the selection of stories in this book, may you be challenged by the faithfulness of these martyrs to live your life "faithful unto death."

CHAPTER ONE

"There Has to Be Something Better"

Ravenna and Milan, Italy—A.D. 99

Martyrs Mirror pages 98-99

Vitalus walked proudly down the street of Milan, his new armor gleaming in the evening light. *It was hard work,* he thought. *But I did it!* He had finally reached the rank of a Roman knight.[1]

Smiling to himself, he entered the courtyard surrounding his home. His wife Valeria, hearing the key in the gate, came to the door. "I did it!" Vitalus greeted her joyfully. "I'm a knight now!"

---

[1] To set the stage for the *Martyrs Mirror* account, this story has more fiction than most. The key facts, however, are as they are given in the *Martyrs Mirror*.

Valeria smiled at his excitement. "I knew you could do it," she said. "You're so brave and good in everything you do."

"And I have more great news!" Vitalus exclaimed. "Judge Paulinus has chosen me to accompany him on his assignment to Ravenna."

Valeria stared at her husband. "You mean we will move to Ravenna?"

"Yes, that's the plan," Vitalus answered. "We will have a lovely place to live, and I will serve in Paulinus' court. Think what an honor it is to have been chosen to go with him."

"But what about our home here?" Valeria's voice faltered. Suddenly her home was very dear to her.

"We can find someone to rent it," Vitalus assured her. "Someday we might come back. Maybe one of the children would like to live here while we're gone."

◆

"This assignment here in Ravenna is not as great as I thought it would be," Vitalus told Valeria as the two lingered over supper. "Today Judge Paulinus sent me to arrest some of those Christians I've been telling you about. Those people are so different! They willingly allow themselves to be arrested. Sometimes they even sing while being led to prison!"

Valeria shook her head. "That does seem strange. What makes them so different?"

"I'm not sure, but I'd like to find out," Vitalus said. "Even when they are arrested, they just radiate peace and joy! I don't understand it."

He lapsed into silence for a bit before continuing. "Today I had to arrest a local doctor named Urticinus. Someone said he was the best doctor around. I felt like a traitor when I led him away. His neighbors just watched sorrowfully. He is to appear before Judge Paulinus tomorrow afternoon."

Vitalus sighed. "My master is a hard man. He is determined to put to death every Christian in the region. And these people don't have a chance once he gets hold of them. But even so, their number keeps growing! As soon as you think you have them all, more appear! It doesn't make sense. Why would more and more people join them if they are wrong?"

"You must find out more," Valeria urged. "Maybe they have the answers to life! There has to be more than what we have known. I always feel so empty."

"I know," Vitalus said thoughtfully. "I thought becoming a knight would be a wonderful thing. I worked hard and was sure it would bring satisfaction. And it did, sort of, for a time. But now when Paulinus sends me to arrest the Christians, I wonder if I made a mistake. There's no joy or satisfaction in getting people killed!" His last words came out bitterly. "There has to be something better—and I intend to find it." Vitalus rose from the table, his face troubled.

The prison was silent as Vitalus walked stealthily down the corridor. Although he had been in this prison dozens of times leading prisoners, this morning he felt out of place. His heart pounded wildly, and he was sure the men in every cell could hear him as he walked along.

He paused as he reached the cell where Urticinus had been confined the day before. *Dare I do it? What if Paulinus finds out?* The memory of his conversation with Valeria flashed into his mind. His own words, "I intend to find it," gave him courage. He inserted the key into the lock and opened the door.

Urticinus sat on his bed, his eyes closed and his hands folded. Vitalus knew instantly he was praying. He hated to interrupt, but he had to find out.

"Urticinus!" His whisper was quiet but urgent. The man on the bed jerked his eyes open and stared in surprise.

Vitalus moved closer. "I am Vitalus, a knight in Judge Paulinus' court. I am the one who arrested you. But I have felt like a traitor ever since!" He paused to get his breath. "I have arrested many of your people because my master demanded it, but I find no pleasure in doing it. Why do you willingly allow yourselves to be arrested? How can you sing while being taken to prison? What makes you so different?" The words tumbled out of Vitalus' mouth.

"Let me answer your questions, my friend," Urticinus said gently. "It is Jesus who makes all the difference. He is my Savior, my Friend, my Lord. He gives joy even in suffering."

"But how?" Vitalus asked. "How can I have the peace and joy you and the other Christians have? What must I do?"

"Believe on the Lord Jesus Christ, and thou shalt be saved," Urticinus quoted. "For God so loved the world, that he gave his only begotten Son, that whosoever believeth in him should not perish, but have everlasting life."[2]

Vitalus listened eagerly as Urticinus explained God's plan of salvation. Occasionally he interrupted to ask questions. Finally he said, "I must leave before I am discovered. But you have given me much

---

[2] Acts 16:31; John 3:16

to think about. I know deep in my heart that you have told me the truth. But I must think about it more—I must be sure." He rose to leave, but then he suddenly turned back to Urticinus. "Can you…Can you forgive me for bringing you to this awful place?"

"I forgive you freely, even as Christ forgave me. And He has the same forgiveness waiting for you. I pray you will find it."

Vitalus couldn't speak. He gripped Urticinus' hand for a long moment, then slipped out of the cell.

Vitalus stood at attention as Judge Paulinus called the court to order. Urticinus, calm and composed, stood before the judge.

"Urticinus," Judge Paulinus spoke, "it is reported that you have turned away from the sacrifices of the gods and are following a way of heresy."

"It is true that I no longer sacrifice to your gods," Urticinus answered. "I worship and serve the true God, the Creator of heaven and earth."

"You serve a false God," Paulinus snarled. "Who are you to tell me what is right? I rule over you."

"There is One who rules over me—God," Urticinus replied. "As God said through the prophet Isaiah, 'I am the Lord, and there is none else.'"[3]

"Do you think you can preach to me?" Paulinus shouted. "I follow the laws of our great Emperor Nero."

"I obey the laws of the King of kings," Urticinus replied quietly.

"I'll make you change your mind," Paulinus growled. "You'll wish

---

[3] Isaiah 45:5

you had never heard of your God. I have no mercy for the likes of you." He motioned to the men waiting at the back of the courtroom.

The men came forward and seized Urticinus. They pulled him to a side room and began beating him.

Vitalus shifted his position. He couldn't see into the torture chamber where they had taken Urticinus, but he knew what was there. The rack. Whips of many kinds. Hooks. Pincers. Torches. He also knew that the cruelty of these men knew no bounds.

Although Vitalus had not yet embraced Urticinus' faith outwardly, in his heart he knew it was what he wanted. He felt a kinship with the man in the torture chamber.

When Urticinus was finally dragged back to the courtroom, Vitalus nearly gasped. Urticinus' back was raw and bleeding, and his clothing was hanging in shreds. But what most caught Vitalus' attention was the look of peace and joy on his face.

"Are you now willing to return to the sacrifices of our gods?" Paulinus sneered.

Urticinus answered without hesitation, "I continue to hold fast to my faith in the one true God."

"Then hear your sentence," Paulinus growled. "Since you remain obstinate, you shall be taken outside the city and your head chopped off with an ax."

Urticinus trembled at the dreadful sentence. For a moment he seemed to waver, as though trying to determine if his God was truly worth dying for.

Vitalus observed all this as he guarded Urticinus. As if compelled by an unseen hand, he stepped closer to Urticinus and said in a low tone, "My dear brother, as a physician you often restored the sick back to health. But take heed now, lest by denying Christ you plunge yourself into eternal death."

Urticinus straightened his shoulders and his trembling ceased. Joy returned to his features at the admonition given. Vitalus breathed a silent sigh of relief.

As the executioners led Urticinus out to kill him, Vitalus stayed behind. He could not bear to watch the execution. When his shift ended for the day, he removed his armor and left it near the courtroom—along with a note of resignation.

Before going home, Vitalus went outside the city to the place of execution. Tenderly he took up the body of Urticinus and carried it away to bury it. Then he hurried toward home—making one more stop along the way. Nervously he knocked on the door of someone he was quite certain was a Christian.

An hour later he continued his way homeward. He knew now what made Christians so happy—because he had it himself! He had also learned where there was to be a meeting that night, and he and Valeria would be welcome.

Paulinus glared at Vitalus as he spoke. "How is it that you have forsaken your knighthood and the worship of the gods? Is it true that you have become a heretic?"

"I have become a Christian and have joined the church of the true God," Vitalus answered freely.

"Is it true that you encouraged that heretic Urticinus when he was condemned to death?" Paulinus asked. "And by your words you prevented him from returning to the worship of the gods?"

"I scarcely knew what I was doing," Vitalus answered. "But I know now it was the Spirit of God who gave me words and bade me speak."

Paulinus' eyes narrowed. "It has also been reported that you buried that heathen after his death. You are a traitor to our country and our honorable emperor. May the worst of tortures be put to you!"

At these words, several men grabbed Vitalus and led him to the torture chamber. First they laid him on the rack and stretched his body painfully. Then, as he lay there, they began beating him with whips.

Paulinus stood at the door of the torture chamber, watching the suffering of his once loyal knight. After some time, he called for them to cease the tortures so he could question Vitalus again. "Are you ready to repent of your obstinacy and return to the sacrifice of the gods?" he asked.

"You must be deprived of your reason," Vitalus answered. "Why should I listen to you and be brought to eternal suffering when I have warned others of this danger?"

A priest standing in the courtroom heard the exchange. "He is hopeless," he told Paulinus. "I advise you to bury him alive and be free of this traitor forever."

"Thus it shall be!" Paulinus decreed. "Carry out the sentence immediately."

Paulinus accompanied them to the execution site. He watched with satisfaction as the men dug a hole and placed Vitalus into it with just his head sticking out. When they had buried him up to his chest, they began heaping up stones and dirt around his head until he was completely buried.

◆

Valeria heard of Vitalus' death from one of the brethren. "There is nothing to keep me here in Ravenna," she said. "My husband is gone, and I would like to move back to Milan to be near my children."

Her old friends in Milan welcomed her back, and in honor of her return, they gathered for a feast. Valeria came to the feast but stayed aloof from the main festivities. At one end of the courtyard was an idol to represent their god Sylvanus. When the food was served, Valeria refused to eat any meat, knowing it had first been offered in sacrifice to Sylvanus.

"Come, take some," a neighbor urged. "It's the best meat around. It's even been made sacred by Sylvanus."

But Valeria shook her head. "I am a Christian. I cannot eat something that has been offered in sacrifice to your god," she said firmly.

"What?" Her neighbor stared at her in disbelief. "You have joined that group of heretics? What ails you?" The conversation caught the attention of the crowd, and others gathered around.

"She says she's a Christian!" one person shouted. Exclamations of dismay ran through the crowd, and they could not be restrained. Their hatred for Christians was intense, and to have one in their midst was unthinkable! Grabbing sticks, they rushed toward Valeria and began beating her. Blow after blow fell until all signs of life had fled. As the crowd dragged her body out of the courtyard, one person muttered, "For the dogs to eat."

The Christians at Milan heard of Valeria's death and gave her a decent burial, mourning the loss of one whom they had just learned to know. But they rejoiced that she had remained faithful unto death.

CHAPTER TWO

"I Have Served My Lord Eighty-Six Years"

Smyrna, Turkey—A.D. 168

Martyrs Mirror pages 112-114

"**B**rother Polycarp! Hurry and let us in!" Urgent knocking accented the words, and Polycarp hurried to unbar the door.

"Come in, my brethren," he invited. "And please tell me why we need such haste."

Two weary men staggered into the room and sank to the floor beside the fireplace. "We ran—" Nicholas gasped. "We ran all the way—from town—to warn you!" He paused to catch his breath.

Peter took up the story. "Brother! You must flee! They are coming for you!"

Polycarp didn't need to ask who "they" were. In his mind he could see them, the town bailiffs and soldiers. They were a rough group of men, heartless and cruel, armed with swords and bayonets. And they had no mercy on those they were sent to arrest.

"I am ready to die," Polycarp said quietly. "We knew this would happen sooner or later. I am prepared."

"No! No!" the men urged. "The church needs you! Come! We will hide you."

Almost against his will, Polycarp allowed his brethren's voices to prevail. He snatched his cloak from the hook and slipped into his sandals. "I will go with you," he said. "Let us go at once."

The two messengers, who had regained some composure, quickly leaped to their feet. Without further hesitation, they escorted the elderly bishop from his home. For the first several minutes, none of them spoke as they rapidly covered the distance from Polycarp's home to a nearby forest.

Once safely in the depths of the forest, the men breathed more freely and Nicholas began to talk. "Remember the group that traveled back from Philadelphia with you? All twelve of the brethren were apprehended this morning."[1]

"Yes," said Peter, "Nicholas and I were in town this morning when the bailiffs brought them in. We stayed in the background but tried to get close enough to see what would happen."

Nicholas spoke again. "I was near the entrance of the amphitheater when I heard the judge order the bailiffs to go get the leader of the group. I knew he meant you, so I hurried to find Peter."

---

[1] This reference to the brethren from Philadelphia is based on the account on page 114 of the *Martyrs Mirror*. These brethren were put to death at the same time as Polycarp.

"We slipped away from the crowd and ran here to warn you," Peter continued. "As we ran, I was praying for an answer. Surely God wouldn't take away our leader! Then God reminded me of the house of Stephen just outside Smyrna. It has an upper chamber where he often keeps guests. I believe God wants us to take you there."

"Quiet!" Nicholas warned. "We are nearing the edge of the forest. We had better wait here until the afternoon sun has set. Then we can safely slip into town and make our way to Stephen's house."

As soon as the shadows of evening began to fall, the three men crept closer to the edge of the forest. "Wait here," Nicholas whispered. "I will go ahead to see if the way is clear."

In a few minutes he was back and beckoned the others to follow him. Silently they made their way across the clearing to one of the back streets of the city. Warm lamplight spilled from some of the windows as they passed.

The three men stopped in front of a large house, and Peter knocked on the door. They waited in breathless silence.

Footsteps sounded inside. "Who is there?" a voice inquired.

"A friend with friends," Peter replied. "Peace be to your house."

In a moment, the door opened before them. "Come in, my brethren, and be refreshed," Stephen said. He smiled warmly as they stepped inside, then closed the door securely and bolted it again. "What brings you to my door this evening?" he asked. "And Brother Polycarp! It is an honor to have you in my home!"

"We have come on an important mission," Peter began hurriedly. "Are we safe here? Is there anyone who can hear us?"

Stephen immediately caught the urgency in Peter's words and sensed the seriousness of the mission. "It is as safe as I can make it," he assured them. "We trust God for the rest."

He gestured to some chairs. "Have a seat, my brethren. I see you are weary."

The three men gratefully accepted the seats, then Nicholas spoke. "Have you heard, my brother, of the apprehension of the twelve brethren that came from Philadelphia?"

Stephen sighed. "I have. May God be glorified through their lives. It is a terrible world we live in—where good is considered evil!"

"That's right," Peter said. "We have come to you, brother, to see if you could host Brother Polycarp in your guest quarters for a while to hide him from the authorities. They are after him—and we need our leader!" He spoke with urgency. "While I was praying on our way to Polycarp's house, the Lord reminded me of your guest quarters. So we have brought him here to stay with you, if you permit it."

Stephen stretched out both hands toward Polycarp. "You are most welcome, my brother. What I have, I share with you. As long as the Lord provides for us, we shall not lack in anything."

Nicholas rose to his feet. "We must head back to the city. I know you will do your best for our dear brother and leader. I can rest easier knowing he is here."

Peter rose to his feet too. "Yes, we must return. But first, let us pray together."

After praying, the two prepared to leave with final words of farewell: "Peace be to this house. God be with you." And Nicholas and Peter slipped out into the night.

Polycarp settled into the guest quarters at Stephen's house and was well cared for. His friends made sure he did not lack any necessities. Stephen often reminded him that he should make himself at home.

One day Stephen handed Polycarp a sealed roll. "Brother Polycarp, here is a letter for you. One of the brethren dropped it off."

Polycarp broke the seal and spread the letter on the table.

> I know thy works and tribulation, and poverty… Fear none of those things which thou shalt suffer… Be thou faithful unto death and I will give thee a crown of life.[2]

Polycarp dropped to his knees and began to pray. He was burdened for the souls of his church brethren. Persecution was already strong around Smyrna. How much more would they have to suffer? "O Lord," he prayed, "help us to be faithful."

His prayer ended abruptly as he fell asleep. Suddenly his pillow burst into flames! In a moment it was consumed.

Polycarp awoke with a start. *Oh, it was just a dream!* he thought with relief. *But it sure seemed real. Is God using that dream to tell me my death will be by burning? My enemies will soon find me, and then death is certain. But then I can see my Savior face to face!* Polycarp's face brightened at the thought.

Three days later, Polycarp looked out his upstairs window to see a group of bailiffs approaching the house. *My time has come,* he thought as a loud knocking sounded below. For a moment he looked at the outside door of his room. *I could easily escape through that door and flee to the neighbor's house. But no, the will of the Lord be done.* With firm steps, he left the room and descended the stairs to meet his captors.

---

[2] Revelation 2:9-10

"Welcome," he said kindly as he opened the door. "Come in and refresh yourselves."

His captors shuffled uneasily. "Why all this haste just to arrest an old man!" one man muttered. They slowly followed Polycarp into the room.

Polycarp immediately prepared a meal for the men. When all was ready, he urged the men to sit down and partake of the food. "Please give me one hour to pray undisturbed before you take me away," he begged. The men looked at each other. Then the head bailiff turned to Polycarp and nodded his assent.

Polycarp withdrew to a private room for communion with his heavenly Father. The hour passed swiftly as he reflected on his life and commended his church into God's care.

When the hour was up, Polycarp went back to the room where his captors were waiting. Immediately they surrounded him and led him outside where they had a donkey waiting to take him into the city.

As they neared the city, two high-ranking officials came to meet them. "Come and ride in our carriage," they invited Polycarp.

Once seated in the carriage, the men began questioning Polycarp. "Why do you not honor the emperor and offer sacrifices to him? If you do, we will save your life."

Following his Lord's example, Polycarp answered nothing. Finally the men demanded he answer them.

"I will never do what you are asking me to do," Polycarp said firmly.

Enraged, the men picked up Polycarp and threw him over the edge of the carriage. Although his leg was injured in the fall, he got up and willingly let the bailiffs lead him to the place of his execution. His injured leg throbbed with pain, but he walked rapidly as if nothing was bothering him.

The group soon arrived at the amphitheater where he was to be executed. Polycarp glanced around the crowd and recognized many of his brethren mingling with the throng, including Nicholas and Peter. Their presence gave him courage. But for their own safety, he did not dare acknowledge them.

Suddenly Polycarp heard a voice. "Be strong, O Polycarp! Be valiant in your confession and in the suffering that awaits you." No one nearby seemed to have spoken the words, and only the Christians gathered around heard the voice.

It was a message from God! A voice from heaven! A thrill of joy shot through Polycarp. God would help him bear what lay ahead.

Then more questioning began. "Don't you value your life, old man? Just give up your beliefs, and we will spare you."

"I have served my Lord eighty-six years, and He has never done me any harm," Polycarp replied. "How could I deny the One who has redeemed me and preserved me from all evil?"

"I'll have the wild beasts tear you to pieces," the proconsul threatened. "They are just waiting to devour you."

"Let them come; I am not afraid," Polycarp responded. "I will not change my mind."

"Then I will have you burned with fire," the proconsul threatened further.

But Polycarp remained unmoved. "Your fire will only burn for an hour. God's fire of judgment on the ungodly will burn forever. But why do you delay? Bring the beasts or the fire, whatever you choose. Neither of them shall move me to deny my Lord."

The waiting crowd was becoming restless. "Kill him!" they shouted.

The proconsul, without further questioning, turned to the executioner. "Burn him," he ordered.

As the executioner prepared to nail him to the wood, Polycarp spoke, "He that gives me strength to endure the pain of the fire will also strengthen me to hold still in the fire."

The executioner stared at him. Was this man insane? Did he not know what death by fire would be like? Nevertheless, he gave the order to just tie Polycarp's hands behind his back. After doing this, the men laid him on the prepared wood.

Immediately Polycarp began to pray. "O Father, I thank you that you have called me to this day and hour and have counted me worthy to partake in Christ's sufferings. I pray that you would this day receive me. I thank you and praise you. To you be glory now and forever. Amen."

Scarcely had he finished praying when the executioner lit the wood under him. As the flames circled around him, the onlookers became agitated. The fire wasn't even burning him! What kind of man was this? Was he some sort of god that possessed magic? A few people began to leave, uneasy about the turn of events.

"Pierce him with a sword!" the proconsul commanded.

Without hesitation, the executioner thrust his sword into Polycarp's side. The blood flowed freely, nearly extinguishing the flames. Silence fell on the crowd. Would the raging fire be extinguished by this man's blood? It was unreal. But then the flames slowly revived, and the crowd breathed a collective sigh of relief.

As the fire finished devouring the body, the crowd slowly dissipated. "Brother Polycarp was faithful to the end," Nicholas murmured as he and Peter moved away from the square.

"He sure was," Peter replied, his voice filled with emotion. "May we likewise be faithful when our turn comes."

"I Have Served My Lord Eighty-Six Years"

CHAPTER THREE

"I Am a Christian"

Lyon, France—A.D. 172

Martyrs Mirror pages 115-116

"Are you coming to the amphitheater this evening?" sixteen-year-old Justus asked his friend Florian.[1]

"I sure am," Florian replied. "And I wouldn't miss it for anything. I heard they have more of those Christians to feed to the wild beasts."

Justus nodded. "I was at the trial this morning, and you could never

---
[1] This story incorporates several different accounts from the *Martyrs Mirror* that took place at the same time and place. It is also written more from the perspective of the onlookers. For some, observing these things raised questions that brought them to the true God.

guess what happened!"

"Tell me," Florian begged.

"Well," Justus began, "they brought in a group of prisoners, and the judge began questioning them. He asked them why they don't worship our gods or obey the orders of the emperor.

"One man—they said his name was Attalus—seemed to be the leader of the group. At least he was the one who talked. He admitted that they don't worship our gods. He said they only worship the one they call the true God."

Florian nodded. "That's what they all say."

"He also said something about not following the emperor's laws if they go against the teachings of their God. The judge tried to put him in his place, telling him he was unlearned and ignorant—that he couldn't possibly know what God wants.

"The judge then asked why they don't attend our worship services as the emperor has commanded. And Attalus, as calm as could be, started quoting things he said were words from God. He said it's sinful to bow down to our idols.

"About this time I noticed Alexander, the judge's right-hand man and physician. He was making strange motions with his hands, and I couldn't figure out what he was doing. Others saw it too. People starting talking to each other until the judge had to call for order.

"One of the onlookers cried out that Alexander was communicating with signs to the prisoners! A soldier confirmed that it was true, so the judge asked Alexander what was going on. I clearly heard Alexander reply, 'I am a Christian.'"

Florian's mouth dropped open. "Alexander a Christian? Imagine that!"

"Yes, and the judge was furious!" Justus continued. "I suppose I would be angry too if my chief servant turned into a heretic! He told the soldiers to put Alexander with the other Christians. He then ordered them all to be thrown to the wild beasts.

"The Christians were all herded out into the courtyard where the soldiers began torturing them. They gave Attalus the most brutal treatment because he seemed to be the leader. After beating him thoroughly, they put him in an iron chair and roasted him over the fire. But they didn't kill him. They plan to execute the whole group tonight."

"What about Alexander?" Florian asked. "I would think he would deserve the worst of tortures since he betrayed his master like that."

Justus nodded. "I couldn't see what they did with him, but maybe we'll find out tonight."

Later that evening the boys were among the crowd gathering in the amphitheater. "Ready for some excitement?" Justus asked.

Florian nodded. "Yes, let's watch the beasts destroy these heathens!"

The crowd jostled for the best spots around the arena. Justus and Florian found a place where they could easily watch the proceedings.

Suddenly the gate opened, and a group of people were dragged into the arena. Some had been beaten so badly they couldn't walk.

"See that man they are carrying? The one that looks so burned and bruised? That's Attalus," Justus told Florian. "But I don't see Alexander. Maybe they decided to keep him for later."

"Or maybe they have already killed him," Florian said. "That's what he deserved."

The soldiers then withdrew, and the gatekeepers released six lions. The boys held their breath as they watched. Quietly the lions padded into the arena and looked around at the crowded bleachers. Several sniffed here and there like curious kittens as they wandered aimlessly through the arena.

"What's wrong with the beasts?" Justus cried. "Usually they can't wait to get to their food. But tonight they don't even act hungry!"

"Oh, look!" Florian said. "That one saw the people now. It's headed toward them!" The boys tensed with excitement. But then they gawked with disbelief as the lion stopped and turned away.

The crowd began yelling at the lions. "Go get them! Eat them up!" But the lions paid no attention. Several lay down and stretched their heads out on their paws. Another sat down and lazily scratched himself.

The crowd grew more and more bewildered. "What's going on?"

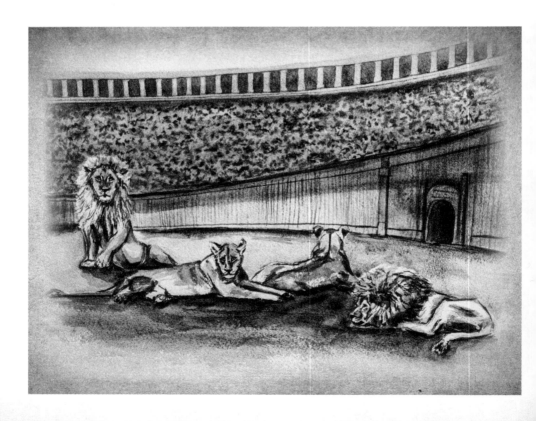

they asked each other.

Finally the gatekeepers entered the arena and herded the lions back to their cages. The boys watched as the soldiers then reentered and drew their swords. Before long, the lifeless bodies of the Christians were scattered around the arena.

The crowd dispersed, disappointed at the turn of events. "Come back tomorrow!" someone called out. "They said Alexander will be killed in the morning."

The next morning the boys were on hand when Alexander was brought into the courtyard. "Maybe they'll roast him too," Justus said. "Did you hear they caught four more Christians last night? Two men and a woman, along with her son."

"As troublesome as they are, these people at least afford us some excitement!" Florian chuckled.

"They sure are strange," Justus said. "I don't know what ails them. I sure wouldn't want my body branded like that." He nodded toward Alexander, where several tormentors were applying red-hot plates to his already beaten body.

Alexander, despite the treatment he was receiving, had a calm, almost serene, look on his face. "He acts like it doesn't even hurt!" Florian exclaimed. "These people must be possessed with some magical powers."

"That has to be the case," a man who overheard him spoke up. "No human in his right mind would let himself be treated like that just because of someone they call God."

As the morning wore on, the torturing continued. Finally the climax was reached, and with the flash of a sword, Alexander's life was over.

"I thought they were going to put him in the arena!" Florian exclaimed.

"Maybe they were reluctant to do it because of how the lions acted last night," Justus suggested.

"I wanted the excitement of the lions," Florian complained.

"The games start tomorrow," Justus reminded him. "That will bring some fun. And maybe they will bring in that new group of Christians. I can't wait to see what happens."

The next morning when the boys entered the courtyard, they were surprised to see the executioners already busy. A woman stood in the middle of the group while several men beat her cruelly with whips. To the side stood a young lad who appeared to be about fifteen years old.

"Look at that boy! He's even younger than we are!" Justus told Florian. "I wonder if that's the lady's son."

Suddenly a voice rang out in the courtyard. "I am a Christian!"

The boys jerked to attention and looked at each other. "Who said that?" they both asked at the same time.

"I think it was the woman," a bystander said. "She has said it before. I think her name is Blandina."

By now Blandina was lying on the ground as the whips continued to cut her. One of the executioners brought a hot plate from the fire and held it against the raw wounds of her body. Then another dragged her over to the rack and fastened her to it.

"I am a Christian!" her voice rang out again. The day progressed with more tortures until it seemed her life should have fled. The executioners mopped their faces. They were getting tired of the effort to make this woman give up her faith. Every time it seemed she was almost dead, she would cry out, "I am a Christian!" That seemed to revive her.

On the other side of the courtyard, another group of authorities was gathered around the two men who had been taken prisoner. Florian and Justus moved back and forth between the two groups.

"What is your name? Who are your parents? Where are you from?" The questions were being addressed to the one who was a deacon named Sanctus.

"I am a Christian," Sanctus replied. "That is my name, my parentage, and my country. Indeed, I am nothing else than a Christian."

"We'll teach you to talk like that!" the tyrants around him raged. They seized red-hot iron plates and applied them to his stomach, his back, and his sides—until his whole body was one big wound.

But Sanctus remained undaunted. "My Lord comforts me and tempers the heat from your fire so I don't feel it."

Maturus, the other prisoner, was being treated in much the same way, but he too remained steadfast.

"These people are impossible!" one executioner exclaimed.

"Take them back to the prison," the judge ordered. "Tomorrow they go to the arena if they don't give up their foolish notions." The three tortured prisoners were dragged mercilessly back to their cells.

The next morning the two friends were on hand again to see the day's happenings. The three adult prisoners, scarcely recognizable from the tortures of the day before, were brought forth, and the young lad was escorted out as well.

"I wonder why they haven't done anything to him?" Justus remarked. "He's a fine-looking young man even if he is a Christian. Too bad he got caught up in that false religion."

The executioners, fresh from their night's sleep, picked up various whips, each selecting a different kind. One by one the prisoners were surrounded and flogged, cutting their flesh dreadfully. Meanwhile, the crowd of onlookers kept growing.

"Let's roast the two men," one executioner called out. Iron chairs were produced, and the men were fastened into them. They were then placed over the fire in the presence of all the spectators. Their flesh, which was severely lacerated, burned quickly.

"How can they still be alive?" Justus gasped. Despite the brutal treatment, the two men's eyes still glowed with peace and hope. Finally the executioners seized their swords and beheaded them.

"We'll save the woman for the last day of the games," the judge announced. The crowd cheered at the prospect.

On the last day of the feasting and games, Blandina and her son were once again brought from prison. "Young man," the judge began, "you have seen what happens when people don't obey the laws of our great emperor and refuse to worship our gods. You can spare yourself if you will only bow down and worship our gods. Your mother will also be set free if she worships with you."

The young lad spoke up boldly. "It is true that I have seen what happens to those you view as heretics. But I am a Christian and will not bow down to any god but the true God." His words so enraged the tyrants around him that they seized him and began beating him mercilessly. So brutally was he treated that his life fled at the hands of the evil men.

Blandina cried out for joy at her son's death. "Thank God he was faithful to the end!" she exclaimed with a happy leap.

Justus and Florian looked at each other. "Is she crazy?" Justus asked.

The executioners grabbed Blandina. "You're next!" they shouted. They dragged her over to a gridiron and grilled her body over a slow fire. Then they wrapped a net around her and headed for the amphitheater. The watching crowd grew delirious with excitement as three wild bulls were released into the arena.

When Blandina was cast before them, the bulls, unable to get to her because of the net wrapped around her, caught her with their horns and tossed her into the air. When she crashed back to the ground, the process was repeated. The crowd howled with excitement as the helpless woman was tossed into the air again and again.

When at last the bulls were done playing with her and had been returned to their pens, two executioners entered the arena to remove the body. "She's still alive!" a man in the crowd exclaimed.

"Cut her throat," the judge ordered. This was quickly done, and Blandina's sufferings were over.

The two friends left the amphitheater together. *I wonder what makes these people so strange,* Florian mused. *Why do they let themselves be treated like this? Who is this God they serve?* A strange longing rose in his heart as he thought of everything he had witnessed the past few days. Blandina's words kept echoing in his mind: *"I am a Christian!"*

CHAPTER FOUR

"Bury Me With the Fetters"

Antioch, Turkey—A.D. 254

Martyrs Mirror pages 134-135

"**O**pen in the name of the law!" an authoritarian voice rang out, breaking the solemn reverence of the worship service.

Fear clutched at every heart as all eyes turned toward the door. Babylas, the bishop of the church, stopped reading and looked up. Silence reigned. No one moved.

Loud pounding on the door came again. "Let us in!" a voice demanded.

Babylas moved calmly toward the door. "Fear not, little flock; for it is your Father's good pleasure to give you the kingdom." His steady voice brought comfort to his congregation.

"Who is there?" Babylas asked as he approached the door.

"The Emperor Decius desires entrance into your church," a voice responded.

In a flash, Babylas thought of his congregation, still sitting there. What would the entrance of this man do to his dear people? His shepherd heart ached for them.

"But you have blood on your hands!" he replied boldly. "This is the house of the living God. It is not right for you to view the mysteries of God with your polluted eyes."

"How dare you speak to me like that?" The emperor's voice came menacingly through the door. "I am the emperor. I demand entrance." With that, a tremendous blow burst the door open. At the same moment, three young men rose from their seats and hurried to stand beside their father.

"Seize these men," Decius ordered. "They will learn not to speak against my wishes."

In moments, Babylas and his three sons were bound together by chains.

"March!" came the terse command.

Mechanically Babylas and his sons obeyed, leaving behind a stunned, leaderless congregation, all of whom quickly scattered to the safety of their homes.

"What do you think they will do with us?" Urban asked in an undertone, hoping their captors wouldn't hear.

"I don't know, my son," his father replied. "But we must be prepared to die."

The group soon reached the prison. "Put these men in the dungeon," the emperor snarled. "Tomorrow they will find out the punishment for their folly."

Down, down, down the guard led the men, coming to a stop before a door deep underground. The guard pulled a key from his pocket and inserted it into the lock. The door creaked open.

"Bury Me With the Fetters"

"Get in there!" The guard roughly shoved the chained men into the dungeon and closed the door.

There was nothing to see—only pitch-black darkness surrounded them.

"We are in prison," Philidian stated, as though trying to convince himself it was real.

"And in a dungeon at that," Epolonius added. "It's so dark I can't see anything!"

The four began feeling their way around the small cell. It was challenging to move, being still chained to each other. Something rustled underfoot. "They must have straw on the floor," Babylas surmised.

Finding nothing in the cell to sit on, the men decided their only option was to sit on the floor.

"Our Lord had not where to lay His head," Babylas reminded his sons. "Even as a baby, His cradle was a feed trough. Surely we can endure this lowly place."

The men conversed quietly for a while, each expressing his personal faith and belief in God. "I tremble at the thought of what we may face," Urban confessed. "But I know God will provide grace to be faithful."

Epolonius spoke. "I rejoice to be counted worthy to suffer for Christ. True, I fear the bodily tortures that might come, but to me to live is Christ and to die is gain!" His voice rang triumphantly through the darkness.

The hours ticked by slowly as they shared Scriptures, sang, and prayed together. They had no way of knowing what time of day it was. Or if night had fallen and it was time to sleep.

Finally the door creaked open and the jailer entered, carrying a pitcher of water and a plate with some bread. "Here's your supper," he said curtly, setting the items down near them. Then he backed hastily out of the dungeon and locked the door again.

Once again the men were in pitch darkness. Babylas felt through the darkness to where the plate of bread was. Picking it up, he said, "Let us thank God for this wonderful provision of bread."

Following the prayer, Babylas passed the plate through the darkness to the others. There were just four pieces of bread, one for each of them. It was dry and almost tasteless. Nevertheless, the men ate their food with gratefulness. The pitcher of water was likewise shared among them.

"Now," Babylas said after the meal was over, "let us once again commit ourselves to our heavenly Father and try to get some rest, that we may be refreshed for what the morrow may hold."

The night was wearying. The men made themselves reasonably comfortable on the floor, but their sleep was restless at best. Unusual noises awakened them from time to time, and the scratching and gnawing of rodents disturbed their dreams.

The arrival of morning brought the jailer to their cell again. Breakfast was a repeat of the previous night's supper. This time, however, the jailer waited. "Hurry and eat," he growled. "You must come with me." He stepped outside, leaving the door ajar. The small glimmer of light from the jailer's lantern was a welcome sight as the men quickly ate the dry bread and washed it down with water.

"Come on," the jailer soon demanded. "It's time to go." The men gulped the last bites, scrambled to their feet, and followed the jailer up the long flight of steps.

"Remember our Lord's actions when He was falsely accused,"

Babylas softly admonished his sons. "May we not bring shame to His name!"

They reached the courtyard and were led across it to the judgment hall. There they came before the judge. It was a mock trial. The emperor's decrees already declared the Christians guilty and worthy of the worst imaginable death if they refused to give up their faith.

The questionings, coupled with various forms of torture, lasted most of the day. All four men remained unmoved despite the pain that racked their bodies.

Toward evening, the judge gave the verdict: "Inasmuch as Babylas, Urban, Philidian, and Epolonius refuse to renounce Christ and return to the worship of the gods of this city, I hereby decree that they shall be put to death with the sword one week hence."

Then the men were led back down the long flight of stairs to the dungeon again. No one spoke for a long time. At last Babylas broke the silence, quoting comforting Scriptures that soothed their hearts.

The following days passed uneventfully. Once or twice a day, the jailer arrived with bread and water, the only physical sustenance they were allowed.

The day before the execution, the men were transferred to a prison cell on the ground level of the prison. Word of the upcoming execution had reached their brethren. To the prisoners' delight, several brethren and friends came to visit them. They enjoyed a refreshing time of sharing and worshiping God together.

"My last request of you," Babylas said as their friends prepared to leave, "is that you bury me with the fetters and chains that have bound me."

The next day as the four men were led forth to the place of

execution, Babylas began to sing the comforting words of Psalm 116:7-9: "Return unto thy rest, O my soul; for the LORD hath dealt bountifully with thee. For thou hast delivered my soul from death, mine eyes from tears, and my feet from falling. I will walk before the LORD in the land of the living."

When they arrived at the place where they would lay down their lives for God, Babylas begged the executioners, "Let me see the death of my three sons first. Then you can kill me." *Lest they see my death and be deterred or discouraged from dying for Christ,* he reasoned.

While the executioners were executing his sons, Babylas prayed aloud, "Here I am, Lord—and the children whom you have given me." With their father's words ringing in their ears, the three brothers went to meet their Savior. Babylas soon followed.

The brethren in the church, along with Babylas' wife, gathered the bodies of the dead and gave them an honorable burial. As Babylas had requested, they buried their beloved leader with the chains and fetters that had bound him.

But Babylas was forever free. The chains and fetters had no more power over him.

CHAPTER FIVE

"I Feel No Pain"

Smyrna and Ephesus, Turkey—A.D. 254-255

Martyrs Mirror pages 135-137

"**M**eet at the 'cathedral' at high noon."
Maximus felt his pulse quicken, but neither his step nor his face revealed that the passerby had said anything of importance. He glanced at the sun as he continued walking down the road. He would have plenty of time to complete his errands in town before meeting the brethren at noon.

I wonder why we are gathering, Maximus mused as he went about his errands. *Could a distant visitor have arrived with news? Or perhaps a traveling bishop is passing through and will preach for us.* Whatever the reason, Maximus would not miss an opportunity to meet with the brethren. Even though most of their meetings took place at night, a noontime meeting was not unknown. Most of the brethren could get to the designated spot under the guise of going about their daily duties.

Persecution was raging in the region, and the church at Ephesus had not escaped. Maximus knew he could be next. *It seems almost every time we gather, more brethren are missing that have been apprehended for their faith. Someday it could be me…*

One by one the brethren arrived at the designated meeting place. Maximus slipped quietly into the secret spot and joined the rest. "Peace be to you," he murmured to the brother standing beside him. Maximus glanced around the group. *Is everyone here?* He couldn't tell.

Brother Mathias motioned the group to gather closer. It was then that Maximus noticed the letter in his hand. "We have a letter from the brethren in Smyrna,"[1] Brother Mathias said softly. He carefully smoothed the letter and began to read aloud:

> To our dear brethren in the church at Ephesus,
>
> Peace be to each one who wholly loves our Lord and Savior Jesus Christ.
>
> We, the brethren in Smyrna, send you greetings, written by the hand of Eusebius. We rejoice in the grace of God that bringeth salvation to all men, thereby giving us the promise of eternal life! We desire greatly the hastening of the day when that

---

[1] This letter is primarily my imagination but is based off the comment in the middle of the second column on page 135 of the *Martyrs Mirror*.

promise will be fulfilled, as we know you also do.

We desire to share with you that our beloved bishop, Brother Pionius, has met his Lord and Savior. He fought a good fight and kept the faith. Even while in prison, he was an encouragement and strength to the brethren. He remained strong, never wavering in his commitment to our Lord.

We wish to share with you of his death, that you may be encouraged to remain faithful to the end. We know not when it may be the end for any of us. Almost daily we hear reports of one of our brethren being arrested or put to death.

Near the end of his life, Pionius spent much time before the governor to answer the many questions presented to him. Never did he hesitate to answer, speaking freely as the Spirit of God gave him words. He had no fear of death, which the governor noticed. So much so that he demanded of Pionius why he was in such great haste to meet death!

"Death is but an entrance into eternal life," Pionius replied. "I do not make haste to meet death, but life." For truly, he was about to be ushered into eternal life and to receive the crown of glory awaiting him.

"You are a fool!" the governor told him. "You are like those who risk their lives to fight wild beasts in the hope of gaining a prize!"

Pionius was soon sentenced to be burned alive. Several of our brethren were privileged to witness his valiant end. When Pionius arrived at the place of execution, he voluntarily prepared to be burned. He fixed his eyes heavenward and prayed, praising and thanking God for His keeping power that had preserved him to that hour. He then laid himself down on the firewood and stretched out, ready to be nailed fast.

Once fastened to the wood, his enemies again tried to convert him. "If you will but promise to forsake this idea of being a Christian, I will remove the nails and set you free," the executioner said.

"Why would I now turn back from serving Him?" our brother replied. "I feel the nails already. What good would come from removing them?"

He then spoke again to his heavenly Father: "Therefore, O Lord, do I hasten to death, that I may rise the sooner."

The executioners then lifted him on his cross with his face to the east. A great heap of wood had been gathered for his burning. He hung there with his eyes closed so long that some thought he had already died. But he was only praying.

Just as Pionius opened his eyes, the flames shot up to a great height. His countenance brightened with joy and gladness as he uttered his last words: "Amen, O Lord. Receive my soul!" With that, he calmly gave his soul into the hands of God, without the slightest hint of pain.

We pray God that our spirits, as well as yours, will be preserved as blameless as that of our dear Brother Pionius, so that we can meet him again someday and be forever with our Lord.

Farewell,

Your brethren in Smyrna.

There was silence for a few moments after Brother Mathias had finished reading. Then he said, "Let us pray together before we part." With one accord, the brethren dropped to their knees and thanked the Lord for the encouragement of the letter. They prayed fervently for grace to stand faithful as Brother Pionius had done.

Following the prayer, the brethren returned to their homes, each wondering who would be the next to offer his life for the truth.

Maximus walked along the road leading toward the city of Ephesus. His mind was full of the words of the letter he had just heard. *Oh, that I might be found worthy to suffer for Christ and to stand faithful to the end!* His heart's yearning turned into a prayer as he walked along.

As a lone rider on horseback approached, Maximus moved closer to the side of the road and continued walking.[2]

"Halt!" an authoritative voice commanded. Obediently Maximus stopped and turned to face the rider. He immediately recognized him as the city bailiff.

"Who are you, and where have you been?" demanded the bailiff.

"My name is Maximus," he replied respectfully.

"And where are you going?"

"I am returning to my home in the city," Maximus answered.

The bailiff peered at Maximus suspiciously. "Where have you been?"

"I cannot tell you," Maximus replied firmly.

"Cannot tell me?" the bailiff roared. "Well, I know how to make people talk! You are going with me."

The angry man dismounted from his horse and tied Maximus' hands together. Keeping a firm grip on the rope, he got back on his horse and urged it into a trot toward the city. Maximus ran along, trying desperately to keep up.

His mind spun from the sudden turn of events, yet he was at peace.

---

[2] I have tried to portray a realistic scene to tie the two *Martyrs Mirror* accounts together.

Clearly his time had come to answer for his faith. And likely he would have to seal his faith with his death. *Can this really be true? So soon after meeting with the brethren? Have I seen them for the last time in this life?* Many thoughts sprang unbidden into his mind.

"Here is another one of those heretics," the bailiff announced as he led Maximus before the proconsul. "I met him outside the city, and he refused to tell me where he had been. That's a sure sign he's a Christian." The bailiff spat out the words as if they tasted bitter.

"Who are you?" the proconsul demanded.

"My name is Maximus."

"Are you a free man or a servant?"

"I am a free man," Maximus replied. "But I am also a servant of Jesus Christ."

"I see we have another Christian here." The proconsul spoke with a sneer in his voice.

Maximus boldly met the man's gaze. "I am a sinner saved by the grace of God. Apart from Him, I am nothing."

"Do you not know the decrees of our great emperor?" the proconsul asked.

"What decrees?" Maximus asked.

"All Christians must forsake their religion and worship the gods of this nation. Here in Ephesus, we serve the great goddess Diana! No other god is equal to her! Great is Diana!"

"I have heard of the emperor's unjust decree," Maximus replied. "But there is only one God, and I will serve no other."

"You must sacrifice to the gods of this nation," the proconsul insisted. "What the emperor decrees, we must do."

"I offer myself only to the true God," Maximus responded. "He is the One I will obey."

"If you won't sacrifice to the gods," the proconsul threatened, "I will have you tortured in all manner of ways you cannot even imagine."

"I am not afraid," Maximus said boldly. "I have always longed to leave this life and attain eternal life."

The proconsul turned to his soldiers. "Beat him!" he commanded.

The soldiers sprang to obey. Blow after blow fell on Maximus.

"I will release you from these tortures if you will give up these Christian notions and worship Diana," the proconsul promised.

"I will gladly endure these torments for the name of Jesus Christ whom I love and serve," Maximus replied. "He gave His life for me. These torments are as nothing. But if I turn away from God, I will face real and everlasting torment."

"Hang him from the torture stake!" the proconsul commanded the soldiers. "We will torture him until he begs for mercy!"

Immediately the soldiers tied Maximus' hands together and suspended him above the ground, then they continued their brutal treatment with sticks and hooks and pincers. "This is happening because of your foolishness," the proconsul said. "Just agree to sacrifice to Diana, and we will save your life."

"It would be far more foolish to try to save my physical life," Maximus replied. "For then I would lose my spiritual life. I shall not sacrifice to your gods. Your torments do not hurt me. I feel no pain. God's grace is with me. He is bearing the pain for me."

"Then hear your sentence," the proconsul declared. "You shall be stoned! It will be an example to other Christians of what happens when you do not obey the imperial decrees of our beloved emperor." He turned to the soldiers. "Lead him outside the city and stone him!"

After releasing Maximus from the torture stake, the soldiers tied his hands together and began the walk out of the city. A crowd gathered quickly and followed as word spread of the impending execution.

"I thank you, O Father," Maximus prayed as he was led out of the city, "that I have been counted worthy to suffer, and that I can be victorious in this battle over Satan. I commend my spirit into your hands."

Once outside the city, the soldiers pushed Maximus to the ground and retreated a short distance. Full of fury, the soldiers and the crowd began to throw stones at him. Just like Stephen, the first Christian martyr, Maximus laid down his life amid a volley of stones for the honor and glory of his Savior.

CHAPTER SIX

"I Shall Never Deny the Only True God"

Caesarea, Israel—A.D. 259-274

Martyrs Mirror pages 138-143

"The Emperor Valerian has decreed that the Christians shall not assemble together anymore. All must gather at the temples of the gods of the nation. Anyone who disobeys will be arrested!" The messenger looked over the group sorrowfully.[1]

Mamas and his fellow brethren looked aghast at the speaker. Could this be true? Was their respite from persecution over?

---

[1] This story combines several accounts in the *Martyrs Mirror* into one story. The timing of the accounts and the location of the events makes it reasonable to think that these characters likely knew each other.

"But I thought Emperor Valerian was friendly to the Christians!" Alexander spoke up. "What happened?"

"Hasn't his house been considered a church of the Lord?" Priscus asked.

"And didn't we hear that Brother Dionysius was invited to dine with the emperor as a sign of his acceptance of the Christian believers?" Malchus added.

The messenger held up his hand as the questions poured forth. "All this is true," he stated as the brethren fell silent. "But I was told that a sorcerer from Egypt went to the emperor and convinced him that if he tolerated the Christians, he would never prosper.

"Some believe the sorcerer cast some kind of spell on Valerian because he changed so radically from a good, kind emperor to a brutal, bloodthirsty tyrant. Even now in Rome and Alexandria, persecution of Christians is raging. Valerian has become convinced that to become successful, he must sacrifice children to the devil."

The messenger shook his head. "I can't fathom such evil! They say his soldiers tear young children from their parents' arms to perform these abominable sacrifices. Men, women, boys, girls, babies—no one whom the emperor suspects of being a Christian can escape. It seems the more brutal the treatment, the better he likes it! He has become a madman. Many Christians are fleeing their homes and seeking refuge wherever they can find it. Some are going to foreign countries, and others are moving into the wilderness or to caves in the mountains. They are leaving everything behind."

"But when they persecute you in this city, flee ye into another..."[2]

---

[2] Matthew 10:23

Mamas quoted. "How long will it be, brethren, before we have to flee?"

"I'm afraid not long," the messenger said. "I was told of a young man named Paul. He is the sixteen-year-old son of a wealthy merchant and knows several languages fluently. But because he is a Christian, he had to flee to the mountains. There God has provided a cave for him."

Silence descended over the group as they tried to grasp what they had just heard.

"Brethren," Malchus spoke up, "we have enjoyed a few years of peace, and I, for one, was beginning to relax. But with the threat of persecution returning, I realize anew that Satan never relaxes. May we all be faithful!"

"That young man, Paul, challenges me," Priscus said. "If he could give up a life of riches and live in a cave for the cause of Christ, can I not also give up the little I have for the One who gave all for me?"

The brethren continued to share hope and encouragement with one another. After a time of prayer, they parted ways, determined to always remain faithful.

During the next few months, Mamas and his friends met faithfully for worship. At each gathering they shared reports of the latest persecution. "I'm sure it's only a matter of time until our church here in Caesarea is targeted," Alexander said.

"Maybe we are too cautious about sharing our faith," Malchus said thoughtfully. "Does not our Lord say, 'The kingdom of heaven suffereth violence, and the violent take it by force'?[3] Perhaps we need to be bolder in our zeal for the Lord."

---

[3] Matthew 11:12

Some of the brethren nodded thoughtfully. "We have gotten used to being more relaxed. Maybe we don't speak as freely as we should," Priscus said.

Mamas spoke up. "I don't think we want to incite violence. We don't want the authorities to turn against us because of unbecoming words or actions."

"We must pray for wisdom," Timotheus said. "God can help us know what to speak and when. And He is the only One who can give us grace to face whatever comes. The judge here has no mercy toward Christians and has sentenced many in other towns. How our church has escaped so far is truly a miracle!"

The next day brought new concerns. "Brother Timotheus has been arrested!" Alexander gasped as he ran up to Mamas, who was seated on the hillside with his sheep. "We are going to town for the trial. Are you coming too?"

"Do you think it's safe?" Mamas asked, voicing his hesitancy as he rose to his feet. "Won't they catch us?"

"Malchus, Priscus, and I have talked about that," Alexander replied with conviction. "And we feel we should go. We are ready to die if necessary. Of course, we will try to blend into the crowd, but we won't back down in fear if someone questions us."

Mamas nodded in agreement. "You are right, brother. I am ready to die as well." He looked over his flock of sheep. "Life has been good, but God is first. May His will be done! I will put the sheep in the fold and head to town. Lord willing, I will see you there." Mamas began leading his sheep back to the fold.

A large crowd had already assembled at the square, and Mamas easily blended in. *How wonderful to see so many of the brethren here!*

Scattered through the group, Mamas recognized various people from church. For their own safety, they could only briefly acknowledge one another. Carefully he edged his way toward the front of the crowd. From there he could see Timotheus standing before the judge.

He was still too far away to understand the conversation, but the firm expression and upright bearing of his friend told him that Timotheus was not caving in to the questioning. Indeed, there was not much questioning. The judge, upon hearing from Timotheus' own mouth that he was a Christian, gave him little time to speak before pronouncing the sentence: "He shall be cast to the wild beasts!"

As Timotheus was led away, Mamas turned his face toward home. Thoughts were churning through his mind. *Should I stay in the area? Or should I flee?*

A tumult behind him caused him to stop and turn around. The crowd was regrouping in the square. *What's going on?* Mamas hurried back to join the growing crowd.

"Why are you shedding innocent blood?" a bold voice rang out. Mamas started. The voice sounded familiar! He pressed forward until he could see. There, standing before the judge, were three of his friends!

"Don't you know God will judge you for destroying His people?" Alexander asked boldly.

"Yes, you need to repent before you suffer the vengeance of eternal fire!" Priscus added.

The judge's lips curled into a sneer. "Who do you think you are?" he snarled. He turned to his officers. "Away with these men! Throw them to the wild beasts too!" He leaned back in his chair as the soldiers sprang to do his bidding.

Mamas watched helplessly as Malchus, Alexander, and Priscus were led away. Then he turned and started toward home once more. His mind could hardly process what he had just witnessed. *Was it wise for them to confront the judge and give themselves away? Is that really what God wants?*

His thoughts were in a turmoil. *I don't want to accuse my brethren of acting foolishly. Maybe they were right to confront the judge like that. But I don't understand their actions. I guess I need to leave it in God's hands.*

As Mamas headed home, a plan formed in his mind. *I must flee. Tomorrow, before daybreak, I will take my sheep and head for the mountains.*

The next day Mamas settled into life on the mountainside. He had left everything behind when he fled except for his Bible. *And the sheep,* he reminded himself. *They afford me much pleasure in this lonely wilderness. Here I can read God's Word undisturbed. I am one with His creation all around me.* That night Mamas sat in the field among his flock, gazing at the starry heavens and marveling at the majesty of the Creator of the universe.

Years passed, and Mamas stayed in the mountains. *So far I have been undisturbed,* he often mused. *But I wonder how long it can last. Someday I will be discovered.*

Living in isolation prevented Mamas from knowing much about the rest of the world. He did not know that Emperor Valerian had been killed and Aurelian was now emperor. He did not know that Aurelian had given new orders to vex the Christians. Nor did he know that the governor's men had gotten reports of some eccentric shepherd out in the mountains who had tamed even the wild hinds, using their milk to make cheese.

"I Shall Never Deny the Only True God"

But Mamas didn't need to know; he just trusted the One who knew everything. As he sat reading, he carefully caressed the worn pages of the book lying on his lap. *I must study the Word diligently so when I am taken captive, I will have it hidden in my heart. They can take the Bible away from me, but they cannot take it out of my heart.*

With another glance at his contented flock, Mamas dropped his eyes again to the book in his lap and continued reading. So intent was he that he did not notice the soldiers approaching until they were almost upon him.

Startled at the sound of footsteps, he looked up. He knew immediately that what he had feared had come. His peaceful existence was over.

Mamas rose to his feet as the soldiers approached. "Good afternoon," he greeted them courteously.

"What were you reading?" the first soldier demanded gruffly.

"I was studying God's Word," Mamas replied.

"Bah." The soldier spat out the word. "No common man can understand the Bible. Give it to me." When Mamas hesitated, the soldier stepped forward and jerked the book out of his hands. With a few swift motions, he tore it to shreds.[4]

"The proconsul demands that you appear before him," the soldier informed Mamas. Without waiting for a reply, the men seized him and tied his hands behind his back. Then they led him down the mountainside and into the city.

For a fleeting moment, Mamas thought of his flock of sheep left alone on the hillside. *What will become of them?* But he quickly pushed

---

[4] The *Martyrs Mirror* does not say this, but it seems logical to assume that he was not allowed to keep his Bible.

the thought aside. *I don't need to worry about them. My heavenly Father, who is watching over me, can care for them too.*

The soldiers brought him before the proconsul. "Your Honor," the lead soldier said, bowing politely, "we have brought you Mamas, the shepherd from the mountains—the one who tames the wild hinds. We found him reading an abominable book he called God's Word."

"A shepherd—reading?" the proconsul asked in disdain. "No shepherd can read a book. Nor can he tame wild animals. It has to be sorcery." He turned to Mamas. "Confess the sorcery and witchcraft you used to tame the wild animals."

"I am a servant of Christ and know nothing of sorcery," Mamas replied. "But it is true that I lived among the wild animals and they had no fear of me—nor I of them. I would rather live among them than among you, for you refuse to know God. I cannot cease to be amazed that you, who have lived many years and attained much wisdom, are still in darkness and reject the true God. Instead, you worship deaf and dumb idols."

The proconsul's face grew red with fury. "Declare that you will sacrifice to the gods!" he demanded.

"I shall never with my lips or my heart deny the only true God or His Son Jesus Christ," Mamas replied firmly. "If I must suffer for Christ, I consider it a high honor and a great gain."

"Place him on the rack!" the proconsul roared. "We will make him give up his faith."

The executioners hurried to obey. After stretching Mamas out on the rack, they picked up their whips and began scourging him. Then they cruelly pinched his body with iron pincers and applied glowing torches to his sides.

"We will stop these torments if you will renounce your belief in God," the persecutors promised.

"I have trusted God all these years; I will not turn back now. He has never failed me. Even now He is on the rack with me, helping me to bear the pain. He will carry me home."

Seeing that nothing could deter Mamas from his faith, the proconsul commanded, "Pierce him with the three-pronged spear!"

The chief executioner grabbed the long-handled spear and thrust it through Mamas's heart. And just as Mamas had said, the Lord carried his soul to his heavenly home.

CHAPTER SEVEN

"I Am Not So Timid"

Tarsus, Turkey—A.D. 304

Martyrs Mirror pages 181-182

Julitta gazed into the face of her sleeping son. "You are so young and innocent," she murmured. "You don't even know that you're fatherless." A tear rolled down her cheek as she recalled the fateful day of her husband's death.[1]

Emperor Diocletian had issued a public decree following the fire

---

[1] In the *Martyrs Mirror* account, nothing is mentioned of Julitta's husband, but it does say she was a widow. Because of the persecution taking place, it seems logical to conclude that he had been a Christian and was martyred.

in Nicomedia that had destroyed his palace.[2] Although unproven, and definitely not true, enemies of the Christians had declared them responsible for the destruction. The emperor was enraged.

I remember when James brought a copy of the new edict home from town, Julitta thought as she subconsciously patted her son. *Quiricus was only three months old at the time. We had to agree to sacrifice to the emperor's gods or be put to death.*

A scene from several months later then flashed into her mind. It was the pained expression of the church brother who had brought her the news of James's death. "Your husband was faithful to the end," the brother told her.

Julitta had stifled her sobs. "But-but…how did he die? Did they torture him a lot? Did they…burn him? Or behead him?" It had sounded cruel to ask such questions, but she had to know!

The brother hesitated. "I wasn't present," he said slowly. "But I was told they treated him quite shamefully before they finally beheaded him. James was faithful to the end. That's what really matters."

"Yes," Julitta had agreed, "that's what counts."

Julitta's thoughts came back to the present. *I still miss him so much! And though it's hard to stay cheerful and to forgive, God is with me. He helps me in whatever I have to do. Like raising my child alone.* She laid her sleeping son on the bed and went out to finish her washing.

Scrubbing clothes and spreading them to dry under the bright sunshine brought more musings. From her vantage point, Julitta could see a glimmer of water to the west. She knew it was the Mediterranean Sea. To the north were towering mountains. "It's beautiful here," she

---

[2] See *Martyrs Mirror* page 173.

whispered to herself. "But I miss my home back in Iconium."

With the persecution increasing around her home, Julitta had fled along with others from her church, hoping to escape the fate that seemed inevitable if they stayed. She had come here to the coastal town of Seleucia and settled into a home, where she was still struggling to make a living for herself and her son. Washing clothes for other people was hard work, but it provided just enough income to pay for their food, clothing, and rent.

I shouldn't complain, Julitta thought. *At least I have work and can provide for little Quiricus.* He was nearly two years old, and she knew he would soon be old enough to begin wondering why there was no father in their home. Julitta had agonized over how she would

explain his father's absence in a way her son could understand. She wanted him to know what a God-fearing man his father had been and why he had been killed.

But what if I am taken and he is left behind? Who will care for him? The thought that had so often plagued her hit her once again with fresh force, and she felt a sense of panic begin to rise. *What will happen to my little boy? Will he have to grow up as an orphan? Will any Christian people take him and train him in the ways of God?*

"Let not your heart be troubled." The words seemed to come from above. Julitta straightened her shoulders. *Why should I worry? God cares about even the sparrows. He is watching over me and my son. He will take care of us.*

Stories of persecution in other areas reached her almost daily. Many Christians were losing their lives. Just last week someone had told her of a large group of Christians who had been loaded on a ship and taken out to sea. When they were too far from land for anyone to swim back, the ship was sunk.

Julitta finished her washing and returned to the house. Little Quiricus stirred as she entered. Seeing his mother, he wriggled off the bed and toddled over to her. Julitta swung him up and hugged him tightly.

As the days passed, Julitta began to hear rumors that caused her heart to quicken. One day the thing she feared came to pass—persecution reached the little church in Seleucia. Once again Julitta decided to flee. It would be harder this time. At nearly three years of age, Quiricus could walk quite well, but she knew he would get tired quickly.

"I will take only the things we absolutely need," Julitta told Quiricus.

"We must make it look like we are going on a short visit, not moving away for good."

The journey was difficult, but Julitta pressed on, grateful for the help she received from other travelers who offered rides along the way. At last she arrived in Tarsus and looked up the address of some fellow Christians.

The family welcomed her warmly. "Persecution is increasing here as well," the father said seriously. "I don't know how much longer we can escape capture." When he saw the look of disappointment on Julitta's face, he continued, "But take courage, sister. God will provide what we need—whether for life or for death."

"Yes, you're right," Julitta agreed. "God will provide. Sometimes my faith grows weak with the burdens of life. But God has always met my needs."

Julitta had not been in Tarsus long before she learned just how true the brother's words were. Somehow the proconsul had learned that she and Quiricus had arrived from Seleucia. He demanded that she appear in court to be questioned.

"Why did you move here from Seleucia?" he asked. "And where is your husband?"

Julitta paused, unsure how to answer. "My husband is no longer living," she answered simply. "My son and I came here to live with friends."

"Who are your friends?"

Julitta responded politely but firmly. "I do not wish to tell you."

"Aha! I thought so. You talk just like the Christians. You are one of them."

"Yes, I am a Christian," Julitta affirmed.

"Young lady," the proconsul began after a pause, "you know that our great Emperor Diocletian has decreed that everyone must worship the Roman gods or be killed. You are still young, and you also have a child to think about. Please consider your ways and return to the worship the emperor has commanded. I will plead your cause and make sure you are given a good position where you can earn a good living and raise your son in the best city in the land. I will even speak to the emperor on your behalf. Perhaps some young man from his royal house will want to marry you, and you can enjoy a good home again!"

Julitta shook her head. "I am not interested in your offer," she said. "I serve my Lord and Savior, Jesus Christ. He is all I need, and He provides for me. I need no other."

The proconsul looked at her as if she had lost her mind. "Lady, do you not understand what you are saying? If you refuse to worship the gods of the emperor, I will have to sentence you to death! Then what about your son? What will happen to him?"

"God will provide," Julitta answered again.

"You are a foolish woman," he said in disgust. "I just offered you the best in the world, and you refused. We'll see if you think differently once you have felt the sting of the whip."

Throughout the conversation, Quiricus had stood quietly beside his mother, holding her hand. At the mention of the whip, several men came forward and seized Julitta. The proconsul picked up Quiricus to keep him away from the whipping.

As the tough cowhide whips tore into her flesh, Julitta could hear Quiricus' frightened screams as he struggled to escape his captor. "Mama! Mama!" he cried. "I want Mama!" The agony of his cries hurt more than the sting of the whip.

She heard the proconsul trying to calm her son, but little Quiricus was not going to be soothed by this strange man! Suddenly the screams ceased and his frightened sobbing came closer to Julitta. But as he came running up to his mother, he was snatched away again. So great was Quiricus' wailing that the men whipping Julitta stopped to watch what was going on.

Quiricus kicked and screamed and clawed at his captor's face, determined to escape this dreadful person who had taken him away from his beloved mother. By now the proconsul's soothing tone had changed to one of anger. "Stop it!" he bellowed. "I'll teach you to act like this!" Swinging Quiricus by the legs, he flung him down the stone steps leading out of the courtroom.

When Quiricus lay quietly, Julitta knew he was dead. Her heart was crushed—and yet it was also comforted. God had seen fit to take her son home to Himself rather than let him be raised among heathens.

She turned to the proconsul. "I am not so timid as to be conquered by your cruelties. You have killed my son and are torturing me, but these things do not move my spirit. Your threats of fire and death cannot separate me from the love of my God. It will only take me that much sooner to my dear son and my Savior Jesus Christ."

Enraged beyond all reason, the proconsul ordered the tortures to continue. "String her up on the stake," he commanded. He ordered iron combs to be raked over her body to shred her flesh. Then he commanded the men to pour melted pitch over her.

Finally he gave one last command: "Cut off her head." With this, Julitta's suffering ended, and she joined her husband, her son, and her Savior.

CHAPTER EIGHT

"I Will Never Again Give Up My Faith"

Cordova, Spain—A.D. 850-856

Martyrs Mirror pages 243-245

"Aurea!" The distressed voice of her friend Priscilla broke through Aurea's quiet morning meditations. "Aurea! John has been arrested!"

Aurea jumped to her feet. "You mean my brother John?"

"Yes!" Priscilla gasped for breath. "I was in town this morning and saw the bailiff leading him toward the courthouse. I ran all the way here to tell you."

Even before Priscilla finished talking, Aurea had slipped into her sandals. Together the girls hurried toward town. A small crowd had gathered when they reached the courtyard, gasping for breath. The trial had already begun.

"This man spoke evil of our great prophet Muhammad!" one man cried out.

"He claims some man called Jesus Christ is the Son of God," another person accused. "He says Muhammad was only a common man."

A murmur of anger surged through the crowd. "We have no God but Allah, and Muhammad is his prophet!" a voice in the crowd rang out.

"He ought to be killed!" someone near Aurea spoke vengefully.

The judge looked scornfully at his prisoner. "It is a serious thing to blaspheme the holy prophet Muhammad. I sentence you to fifty lashes across the back. The sentence is to be carried out immediately. This will teach you not to blaspheme." The judge nodded to his waiting servants to proceed with the sentence.

John's voice rang out firmly for all to hear. "I will be faithful to God until I die! I am innocent of the evil I am being accused of."

The judge turned to John, his face contorting with anger. "How dare you contradict my judgment? You will be whipped five hundred times or more until you have learned to respect your leaders."

Aurea could hardly bear to watch as the whip cut mercilessly into John's back time and again. She moaned softly as he finally fell to the ground. "Oh, Priscilla!" she whispered. "They have killed him!"

Priscilla placed her arm around Aurea in silent support as the judge ordered the whipping to stop.

"He's still alive!" one of the servants exclaimed after observing

John's body for a few moments.

The judge quickly issued a new order: "Set him backwards on a donkey and lead him up and down the streets of the city. Cry aloud, 'Thus shall it be done with the revilers of our prophet Muhammad.' When that is done, throw him into prison."

"Come, Priscilla, let's go," Aurea begged. "I can't bear to watch anymore."

As the two girls left the city, Aurea could hear the voice of the crier. "Thus shall it be done…"

As the days went by, Aurea often wondered how John was doing. Occasionally messages leaked out from other prisoners, and she would hear bits about him. She was encouraged by word of his faithfulness even while languishing in chains.

But one day sad news reached her. John had died. "No one seems to know why he died," the messenger told her. "Some think he never recovered from the terrible whipping he received. But we know he stayed faithful to God."

"I have been ordered to bring you before the judge." The bailiff spoke in an authoritative tone. "Come with me at once."

"What have I done?" Aurea asked as he bound her wrists together.

"You can ask the judge that," the bailiff sneered. "You people are crazy." He muttered some other words under his breath as he mounted his horse.

As she ran behind the horse, Aurea's mind traveled back over the years. She had been taught about God as a little child, and her life had been relatively pleasant until persecution had started against the

Christians. First her parents had been killed, and then her brother John had died in prison. That had been six years ago. But up to now she had faced no direct persecution herself.

The journey to the courthouse seemed much too short for Aurea. She knew her time had come to suffer for her faith, and her flesh recoiled. When they arrived, the bailiff dismounted and escorted her into the presence of the judge.

"Aurea," the judge's voice was almost kind, "how is it that my own niece stands before me as one accused of wrongdoing? I hear you are part of the Christian religion. Please tell me it isn't so! I don't want to condemn you."

"Yes, I am a Christian," Aurea replied without hesitation.

"But you know there is no God but Allah, and Muhammad was the greatest of all his prophets. Turn back to the religion of your country. Just think of all the pleasures that could be yours. You are part of a noble family and could get married to some important person. You could have servants to do your work for you and have a life of ease."

Aurea remained silent.

The judge spoke again. "If you don't give up your faith, my servants will torture you. They have all kinds of ways to make people change their mind. Sometimes they stretch them on a rack till their limbs are nearly torn from their bodies. Sometimes they whip them over and over. They jab red hot pokers into them. Think about it, Aurea. You will suffer much pain—too much to endure. I don't want to see you suffer like that. Just say the word, and we will let you go free."

Aurea shuddered inwardly at the thought of the horrible torture. Could she stand it? Her mind flashed back to John's torture. She could almost feel the searing pain of the whip lashing her body. No, it would be too painful. She looked at the judge. "I renounce my faith in God," she said. "I will worship Muhammad."

The judge smiled. "You have made a wise decision. I am glad to see that my niece has so much common sense. I will do all I can to give you a good life." With that, he released her from the court.

Aurea walked slowly down the road toward home. She was free! But her heart was heavy. "What have I done?" she groaned. Gone was the peace she had experienced for so many years.

When Priscilla stopped in to share with her about the next meeting, Aurea tried to act as though nothing had changed. But inside, she was sick. Her heart felt leaden. *There's no way I can go to the meeting and face everyone. Someone has surely heard what I did.*

"Aurea, what's wrong?" Priscilla asked in concern. "You don't act like yourself."

Aurea just shrugged and forced herself to smile. "I'm just extra tired," she said lightly. "I'll be fine."

Priscilla looked unconvinced, but after another searching look at her friend, she quietly left.

Dreary day followed dreary day. *Will I ever be happy again?* Aurea wondered. Verses she had memorized came to haunt her. "*There hath no temptation taken you... God is faithful... a way to escape, that ye may be able to bear it.*"[1]

"If only I could stop thinking!" Aurea cried one night as her distraught mind kept her awake. Vivid images of burning in hell marched through her mind.

And then a gentle Voice penetrated the depths of her despair. "You

---

[1] 1 Corinthians 10:13

need to return to me. You must repent of your sin of disowning me. I will not cast you away; I am waiting for you."

Aurea could stand it no longer. "God," she prayed as she fell to her knees, "I have failed you. I have rejected your love. I feared the tortures of men more than I loved you." Tears of repentance fell, releasing the tension of the past days. Aurea prayed for a long time, confessing her weakness and failure and seeking God's forgiveness. She prayed for strength to face whatever lay ahead.

Peace again flooded her being. Suddenly she remembered that the believers were gathering again that night. Renewed by the joy of having her sin forgiven, she no longer felt the weariness of the past days. Although she had missed the first part of the meeting, Aurea couldn't stay home. She hurried to join her brothers and sisters.

At the meeting, Aurea confessed her failure and told how God had worked to bring her back to Him. Her fellow brothers and sisters freely forgave her and rejoiced with her at her renewed commitment to God. "Pray for me that I can remain faithful," she begged.

In the coming weeks, Aurea joined the believers at every opportunity. She drank in the truths that were taught, endeavoring to fortify herself against any further onslaught of the enemy. She knew it was only a matter of time before she would be called before the judge again.

And it wasn't long. When someone informed the judge of Aurea's return to the Christian faith, he immediately sent the bailiff to bring her to him. "What is this I hear about you?" the judge asked. "You told me you would give up your faith."

God's Spirit strengthened Aurea. "I never really forsook the true religion. Yes, I said I renounced my faith in God, but I never did from my heart. I felt miserable until I repented and openly confessed God again. He has graciously forgiven me for my failure to stay faithful. I will never again give up my faith."

"Aurea, how can you do this to me?" the judge asked. "I don't want to condemn you, my own niece! I want to see you get married to an important young man and have a family of your own. You are too young to die! Remember all the tortures I said we use to make people change their minds?"

But Aurea remained firm. "At one time I was weak and feared your tortures. I thought I could spare myself much suffering by pretending to deny my faith. But God has helped me see how wrong I was. Now I see your tortures as nothing compared to the grief I would feel if I turned away from God. Without Him, hell awaits me. And that is eternal torture. Your tortures are nothing in comparison."

The judge shook his head. "Take her to prison," he ordered his servants. "I'll see what the king decrees against her. She comes from a noble family. Maybe he will have mercy."

But the king's command was ruthless. "Kill her with the sword! Anyone who turns away from the holy faith of Muhammad does not deserve to live, whether they be princess or peasant. The only mercy she gets is a quick death. Hang her body by its heels from the gallows as an example to others who think they can forsake the faith of our great prophet."

The command was soon carried out, and Aurea's body, along with that of a murderer, was suspended from the gallows for all to see. She had gone to her reward.

Chapter Nine

"We Worship the True God"

Osca, Spain—A.D. 851

Martyrs Mirror pages 244-245

"No child of mine is going to live under my roof as a Christian! You have twenty-four hours. Either give up your Christianity and join the Muslim faith—or get out." Abdullah spat out the words as he glared at the girls standing before him. Then he turned on his heels and stalked out the door.

"What shall we do?" Aloida asked her older sister as they watched their stepfather striding angrily away from the house. "He is furious. Who knows what he will do if we don't obey him!"

Nunilo hesitated. "I don't know. But we can't deny our faith. Oh, if only Mother hadn't married him after Father died! Father was also a Muslim, but at least he let us live out our Christian faith."

"I know," Aloida sighed. "Mother changed so much after Father died."

"And why did she become so careless about her Christian life?" Nunilo added, voicing a concern that had plagued her for months. "Was she never a genuine Christian? Maybe she was just a Christian because Father allowed it."

"Maybe we could go live with Aunt Claudia!" Aloida suddenly exclaimed. "She's a true Christian. And I know she would welcome us."

"That's a good idea," Nunilo agreed.

Early the next morning, the two sisters gathered their meager belongings and left the house.

Aunt Claudia was surprised to see them. "Why, Nunilo and Aloida! What are you doing here? And why do you have your satchels with you?"

The girls glanced at each other, then Nunilo spoke. "Our stepfather told us we must either follow the Muslim faith or…or leave." Her voice broke.

"I'm so sorry!" Aunt Claudia sympathized. "But do come in and tell me about it. Where are you planning to go?" She led the girls inside.

Between the two of them, the girls told the story. "Could we…?" Aloida said at the end. "Is there any chance we could live here with you?"

"Of course," Aunt Claudia assured them. "I will be glad to have you."

As the two girls settled into their new life, Aunt Claudia faithfully taught them more about the Christian way of life. Nunilo and Aloida once again enjoyed the peace of a Christian home, and their lives blossomed as they put to practice the truths they were learning.

The girls relished every opportunity to gather with fellow believers, although they knew they could be apprehended at any time for their faith in God.

Since they were cut off from their family, Nunilo and Aloida had no idea that their stepfather was still angry with them. They had no way of knowing that he wasn't satisfied with just driving them away from home. Or that he had reported them to the judge.

One day in early September, a messenger reined in his horse in front of Aunt Claudia's house. In his hand, he carried a summons for Nunilo and Aloida to appear before the judge. There was scarcely time to bid Aunt Claudia farewell before they were led away. "Stay true to your Lord," Aunt Claudia encouraged in her hasty goodbye.

When they reached the city, the messenger led them to the courtroom. "Your Honor," he said, bowing before the judge, "as you have commanded, I have brought you the daughters of Abdullah."

The judge acknowledged the messenger and dismissed him with a wave of his hand. He studied the young girls before him. "How is it that you, daughters of a Muslim, have become Christians? Don't you know that the Muslim religion is the only right one?"

"We worship the true God," Nunilo replied fearlessly. "Following Him is the most blessed life anyone can know."

"Obeying our heavenly Father is worth more than anything else," Aloida added.

"Listen, my daughters," the judge said in a fatherly tone. "You have been deceived. If you give up your Christian religion, I'll give you each much money and jewelry. You can be rich! More than that, I'll arrange for both of you to marry noble young men."

"Oh, Judge," Nunilo answered firmly, "how can you ask us to turn from true godliness? No one in this world is richer than our Savior Jesus Christ. Without Him, there is no life. We have given our lives into His keeping."

"You don't know what you are saying. You are young yet. Think of the life you have before you. Riches and pleasure can be yours." The judge leaned back in his seat. Surely the girls couldn't refuse his offer.

"Your riches are as nothing," Aloida replied. "Without Christ, all is vanity."

The judge was shocked and enraged. His fatherly tone was gone. "Then I will have you tortured with all kinds of tortures and have you killed."

"We are not frightened by your threats," Nunilo responded. "Your tortures last but a short time. And if you kill us, we will only go to be with Christ, our heavenly Bridegroom."

The judge was amazed at their calm response. He called two of his servants. "I decree that these two daughters of Abdullah shall be taken to the homes of two respected Muslim women. Nunilo shall go to the house of Masuma and Aloida to the house of Abla. From this time forward, they shall not be permitted to speak to each other or to any other Christian people. They shall be faithfully taught in the ways of Muhammad and all effort made to bring them back to our sacred religion."

The servants obeyed the orders and delivered the girls to their new homes. Every day the Muslim women presented their sinful doctrines and practices to the girls, trying to "save" them from the "heretical" faith of the Christians.

Nunilo's first lesson was how to pray to Allah. "Repeat this prayer after me," Masuma instructed. "There is no God but Allah, and Muhammad is his prophet."

Nunilo remained silent. She refused to join Masuma on the prayer mat provided for her. Instead, she silently begged God to help her be faithful. Every day she remained firm in her commitment to God.

At Abla's house, a similar scenario played out as Aloida refused to participate in any practice that was contrary to God's Word. Day after day, she faithfully resisted the evils put before her.

Nunilo and Aloida were finally brought back to the tribunal. "These girls persist in their stubbornness," the Muslim women said. "We can do nothing with them."

The two girls were overjoyed to see each other again, though they were still not permitted to talk to each other. But just being together and knowing that the other had stayed faithful was a blessing they both cherished.

The judge made one last appeal to turn them from the ways of Christ, but the girls never wavered. "Muhammad is an enemy of Christ. We will never follow his doctrine."

The judge soon gave his sentence:[1] "Take them outside the city

---

[1] From this point on in the story, some of the events are from the next account. Due to the comment in the *Martyrs Mirror* about the differing details of the writers, I have used the account of Emilas and Hieremias to conclude this account. These two accounts are so similar that they could possibly have been the same individuals with different names from different writers. However, it likely was two separate occasions.

"We Worship the True God"

and behead them. Hang their bodies on stakes so all who see them will know what happens when people refuse to follow our holy prophet."

As the girls were led outside the city to the place of execution, the sun shone brightly from the October sky. The execution didn't take long—two swift blows with the gleaming swords and the faithful brides met their Bridegroom.

Suddenly the sky darkened and earthshaking thunder roared through the heavens. Terrifying bolts of lightning flashed to the ground, and a strong wind whipped through the trees. As great hailstones crashed to the earth, men and women screamed and fled in terror for whatever refuge they could find.

The judge, still sitting in his judgment seat, gripped the arms of his chair, his face white. What was going on? Why was there such a tremendous storm in the middle of a sunny day? One servant who managed to stumble back through the storm mumbled something about God judging them for killing innocent people.

The judge relaxed slightly as the sound of the thunder gradually lessened. Surely this was just a coincidence. There must be some natural explanation for this strange phenomenon. Maybe his magicians could tell him what had happened. He would ask them tomorrow. For now, he would say some extra prayers to Allah.

"We Worship the True God"

CHAPTER TEN

"I Will Remain a Christian"

Cordova, Spain—A.D. 922-925

Martyrs Mirror page 256

Ermoigus closed the stable door and turned the key in the padlock. A glance at the western sky told him the hour was getting late. He hurried toward his cabin near the woods that spread out below the king's palace.

"Pelagius, are you ready to go?" he asked as he entered the cabin.

The ten-year-old jumped to his feet. "Yes, Uncle Ermoigus. I have been waiting for you."

Ermoigus smiled at the eager boy. "The work in the stables took longer than I expected this evening. We have to hurry to get to the meeting."

The two figures slipped stealthily into the woods and made their way toward a thicket on the far side of the forest. "Uncle," Pelagius spoke suddenly as they hurried along, "does the king know we are Christians? Today I heard some boys saying the king hates the Christians and wants to kill them. Will he kill us?"

Ermoigus laid his hand on Pelagius' shoulder. "I don't know, my son." His voice was low and sad. "We will trust God to keep us. Even if the king tries to destroy us, God's grace will be sufficient for us to stay faithful. Remember that, Pelagius."

A look of sadness crossed Ermoigus' face. "As you know, your parents were both killed when you were a toddler. Since then, things have been mostly peaceful, but we never know when persecution will strike again. We have been tolerated but not fully accepted. That is why we meet in secret."

Soon the two reached the thicket where the meeting was to be held. The brethren greeted each other quietly but joyfully.

Ermoigus, who served as the bishop, soon began speaking to the group. "'Fear not them which kill the body, but are not able to kill the soul: but rather fear him which is able to destroy both soul and body in hell.'[1] Brethren, I hear that persecution may again be increasing in the region. Let us always remember that God is faithful and will not allow us to be tempted more than we can bear. He will make a way for us. We know not—"

"We found them!" a voice yelled, interrupting the bishop's words.

---

[1] Matthew 10:28

So intently were the Christians listening to the Word being preached that they had failed to notice the approaching soldiers. Quickly the brethren scattered into the trees, racing through the forest to escape. One of them grabbed Pelagius' hand and dragged him along.

"I have the leader!" a voice rang out triumphantly.

Pelagius felt his heart sink. *Uncle Ermoigus has been captured!* It took several moments for the boy to realize that he was not also a prisoner but had been saved by one of the brethren. Brother Philip was pulling him deeper into the forest.

When they were a safe distance away, Philip and Pelagius stopped. In the darkness, they had no way of knowing where the other brethren were or how many had been captured.

"Pelagius," Philip said softly, "you heard the soldiers. Your uncle has been captured."

"I know." Pelagius' voice trembled a little. "What do you think they will do to him?"

Philip's voice was also trembling. "I don't know. But they have little mercy for any Christians. Let's pray together right now for Ermoigus."

Pelagius felt comforted as he listened to the prayer. "We ask, O God, that you would be with Brother Ermoigus as he has been captured by the king's soldiers. We know they have no mercy on your people. Please grant boldness and strength to your servant so he can remain faithful to you."

Philip took a deep breath. "We also pray for Pelagius, who has just lost the one who has been a father to him nearly all his life. We ask that you would be near to him and be a Father to him as you have promised. Give him strength and courage to face the days ahead."

When the prayer ended, Philip said, "I will take you to my house for the time being. My wife and I will be glad to have you."

"Thank you, Brother Philip," Pelagius said gratefully.

Softly the two slipped away into the night and made their way through the woods. Pelagius was glad when they could see the dark outline of Philip's cabin in the darkness.

The tribunal was crowded as the king called the court to order. "Your Honor," the army general said as he stood before the king, "we captured a leader of the Christians last night at a secret meeting they were holding in the woods below the royal palace."

"What?" the king shouted. "Those heretics were meeting on my property? Bring the leader to me. He will answer for such actions."

The general left and soon returned with two soldiers leading Ermoigus, his hands chained behind his back.

"Your Honor," the general spoke again, "we have brought you Ermoigus, the leader of the group. He is one of your stable hands." The general paused momentarily. "The best one, they say." He saluted and stepped back.

The king stared at the prisoner, trying to comprehend what he had just heard. He motioned the soldiers back and beckoned Ermoigus to step closer.

"What is this I hear about you?" the king asked. "Is it true that you are the leader of a group of heretics that despises the law of God?"

"I worship the true God and obey His Word," Ermoigus answered firmly but respectfully. "I know nothing about being involved in heresy."

"Is it true that you gather in secret at night? And that you were meeting on my property?"

"That is true, Your Honor."

The trial continued as the king questioned Ermoigus. The king seemed to find it difficult to come to a verdict. At last he turned to his soldiers. "Take him back to prison. I will speak with him again later."

Ermoigus spent his time in prison praying for his church and his nephew. *What will become of Pelagius? Did he escape? Or was he also captured?*

"O God," he prayed fervently, "be with Pelagius, wherever he is. Strengthen him for whatever he is facing. He is so young! Be a Father to him." Ermoigus felt a sense of peace steal over him as he prayed. Everything would be all right.

A rattle of keys in the lock caught his attention. He looked up as the prison guard and two soldiers entered the cell.

"The king wishes to speak with you again," one of the soldiers said as he snapped a chain onto Ermoigus' wrist. They led him from his cell toward the king's judgment hall.

As they entered the judgment hall, Ermoigus swiftly scanned the group of faces gathered. Joy flooded his being as he noticed Pelagius standing with the onlookers. Some other brethren were also in the crowd.

"Ermoigus, I have an offer to make to you," the king said. "If you will give up your heretical Christianity, I will promote you to being my personal servant. You will care for my horse in my private stable and will be provided a larger home. You will never know any need." The king settled back. This was an offer that couldn't be refused!

Ermoigus didn't hesitate. "I cannot give up my faith in God," he stated firmly. "I will die before I do that."

The king stared at his stable hand. Had he heard correctly? This man would rather die than be promoted to being his personal servant?

Before the king could respond, Ermoigus spoke again. "Your Honor, I ask that you release me to leave this country. I will move out of your kingdom so I may freely serve my God."

"What?" The king shook his head in amazement. "You are asking to be exiled? Do you know what you are saying?" The king was visibly disturbed by the request. He hated the Christians, yet this man unnerved him; he couldn't bring himself to condemn him to death. The only thing to do was to convince him to give up his faith. And now he was asking to be exiled!

"My young nephew Pelagius can remain with you and serve you in my stead," Ermoigus offered.[2]

The king shook his head again. "You are a strange man," he said. But then, almost as though he didn't know what he was saying, he relented. "Your request is granted. I give you three days to leave my kingdom. Your nephew Pelagius shall remain a servant in my kingdom in your stead."

I wonder what happened to Uncle Ermoigus. Pelagius' thoughts roamed back to the day three years ago when his uncle had been banished from the kingdom. *Why did he ask to be released and yet leave me here to live under the king's hand?* Such thoughts had often passed through the boy's mind as he went about his responsibilities around the palace.

Having been assigned to help care for the king's gardens gave Pelagius much time to think and meditate. He enjoyed the work among nature and reveled in the nearness he felt with his Creator. When opportunity afforded, he slipped away and joined his brethren for worship. But the meetings were few because the king's soldiers

---

[2] One cannot understand why a genuine Christian would leave his young nephew in servitude to a wicked king. We have no way of knowing what the reasons were that caused this Christian man to make such an agreement. Did he expect his church brethren to rescue Pelagius? Did he think the king wouldn't keep such a young boy there?

kept a watchful eye on the movements of all the villagers.

"The king requires you to come before him," a councilor ordered Pelagius early one summer morning. The young man straightened up from his work. *My time has come,* he thought as he followed the councilor to the royal hall. Though only thirteen years old, Pelagius had already grown into a fine, well-mannered young man. He was well respected by those who worked with him because of his irreproachable character.

As he stood before the king, Pelagius immediately began to testify of his faith. "I will die for the name of Christ," he declared.

But the king was not interested in a confession from the youth. "I wish to promote you from your service as my gardener," he said. "I need someone young and good-looking to assist in serving at my evening festivities. I have many rich and famous guests, and you would impress them highly. You will be dressed fashionably to serve them." The king continued to talk about the many pleasures Pelagius could enjoy with his change of occupation.

Pelagius, still untainted by many of the evils around him, shuddered at the words of the king. "I cannot take part in such things," he stated firmly. "They are part of the worship of the devil. I would rather die an honorable death in Christ than live a polluted life with the devil."

The king continued to pressure him. "If you give up your Christian faith, I will take you into my court. You can have all the royal splendor you could possibly want. You can be my personal assistant and go with me everywhere I go. You will get to see the world!"

Strengthened by God's Spirit, Pelagius answered boldly, "I am a Christian and will remain a Christian. I have pledged my life to God, and Him only will I serve the rest of my days."

Enraged, the king shouted, "Take hold of him, guards! Torment him until he dies or renounces his God."

The guards suspended him in the air with iron tongs. Just when Pelagius felt sure his arms would be torn from his body, he was lowered to the ground. As his arms flopped helplessly, large pincers were applied to various parts of his body. But Pelagius refused to deny his Lord.

"We will torture you more," the king threatened.

"Though you torture me to death, I will not give up my faith," Pelagius replied fearlessly.

"Then cut him into pieces and throw him into the river," the king commanded.

Pelagius clasped his hands together and raised them to God in prayer. "Lord, deliver me from the hands of my enemies."

The executioners yanked his hands apart and cruelly cut off one arm, then the other. Then they cut off his legs. A final blow removed his head. Gathering up the pieces, they threw them into the river.

God had answered Pelagius' prayer. The young hero was finally delivered from his enemies as his soul went to be with Jesus.

CHAPTER ELEVEN

"If You Can Burn This Flower"

Scharding, Austria—A.D. 1527

Martyrs Mirror pages 420-422

"Yea, and all that will live godly in Christ Jesus shall suffer persecution. But evil men and seducers shall wax worse and worse—"[1] The bishop's words ended abruptly as a knock sounded on the door. Immediately he closed the Bible and handed it to one of the brethren to hide as he got to his feet.

Faces paled as the knock came again. A few brethren glanced

---

[1] 2 Timothy 3:12-13

toward the back door as if trying to decide if they should make a quick escape into the night. "It's not the pounding of the burgomaster," one man whispered reassuringly.

Cautiously the bishop opened the door. Light from the oil lamp cast shadows onto the porch where he could see the form of a man. "How can I help you, my friend?" he asked calmly.

"Have you a place where a weary man can spend the night?" the stranger asked. "I have traveled many days, coming from the town of Scharding. There have been no inns along the way for the last several hours. When I saw the light in your window, something compelled me to stop."

"Step inside," the bishop replied. "I am sure we can find a place for you to retire."

The stranger entered somewhat nervously. "Even a barn would be welcome," he said.

The brethren greeted him cordially. One of them offered his stool for the man to sit on. As he sank down heavily, his weary features became more pronounced in the lamplight.

"You look tired," one of the brethren said. "Would you like a glass of water?"

"That would be refreshing," the stranger replied. "I have had a long journey."

The bishop resumed his seat. "What is your name, friend? And what brings you all the way to Moravia from Scharding?"

"My name is Thomas Mittermaier," the stranger began. "I am the chief servant of the judge of Scharding. Or I should say I *was* his chief servant until last week." He paused to take a drink from the glass offered to him.

The almost imperceptible looks of alarm that had crossed the brethren's faces when the man began to speak now changed to bewilderment. "You say you were the chief servant until last week?" the bishop asked. "What happened to change that? Did you fall out of favor with your master? Are you perhaps fleeing from his anger?"

The man shook his head. "I don't know where my master is now. He resigned from his office and moved away, after…" The man stopped speaking, looking as if some haunting memory had overcome him.

"What happened?" the bishop asked.

"Oh, if you had seen what I saw take place in Scharding last week…" The man stopped again, overcome by the memory. "The scene has haunted me every day since then, and I can't sleep at night. I'd do anything to have the peace that man had!"

"Tell us about it," the bishop urged kindly.

The stranger looked around the circle of men, seemingly counting the cost of sharing his experience with these people. He took a deep breath. "I have to talk to someone! The weight is nearly killing me! I-I know it is dangerous to speak freely of such things, but something tells me I can trust you. You have the same look of peace that Leonhard had."

After another pause, he began his story. "A former priest named Leonhard Keyser was brought before my master on charges of heresy. He had two years earlier joined the group that was called Anabaptists. My master, as well as many other priests and bishops, questioned him and tried to persuade him to give up his faith.[2]

"But Leonhard steadfastly refused. He said he had carefully studied

---

[2] Although the *Martyrs Mirror* indicates Leonhard Keyser was an Anabaptist, other sources say he was a Lutheran. Regardless of his church affiliation, his faithfulness under trial is commendable.

the teachings of the Anabaptists and said their beliefs and practices aligned with the Scriptures. Thereupon our priests, bishops, and my master called him a heretic. They told him he had left the body of Christ by forsaking his priesthood and the state church.

"Leonhard replied calmly that he had found the true body of Christ and could not with a clear conscience remain part of the state church with its false teachings.

"Many times during the discourse, Leonhard requested that they speak in German so the common people who were listening could understand the discussion. But our leaders always addressed him in Latin because they knew he understood the language. Leonhard, however, always answered in German, making it fairly easy for the people to guess what the authorities were asking.

"Leonhard refused to turn back to the state church, so they finally condemned him to die by being burned at the stake.

"Last Friday was a beautiful day. They bound Leonhard onto a cart and took him to the execution site. I rode along beside my master, who was riding beside the cart. The priests were still trying to get Leonhard to recant, speaking to him in Latin.

"The place of execution was in a field just outside the town. As we entered the field, Leonhard did a strange thing. He leaned out of the cart and plucked one of the white wildflowers growing in the field. Then he spoke to my master. 'Lord Judge, here I pluck a flower. If you can burn this flower and me, you have justly condemned me. But if you cannot burn me and this flower, consider what you have done and repent.'

"My master laughed at him, but I could see he was a bit worried. Upon arrival at the fire, he ordered the executioners to pile on extra wood. He even dismounted from his horse to help. I had never seen him do that before! It was as if he was determined to make sure nothing could survive the fire. They had enough wood to burn ten men!

"They used ropes to tie Leonard to a ladder, with him still clutching that flower in his hand. Then they thrust him into the fire. Above the crackling of the flames, we heard Leonhard's voice, loud and clear, praying to God to receive his spirit. When he started praying, the ropes that bound him to the ladder burned off, and then an amazing thing happened. He rolled right out of the fire! The executioners grabbed some long poles and thrust him back into the flames. But then he rolled out the other side! It would have been funny if it weren't such a horrible thing.

"Once the fire burned down to nothing, Leonhard's body was still completely whole. And in his hand was that flower, just as fresh and clean as when he had picked it!

"My master was clearly troubled, but he ordered the men to build an even bigger fire—because this man's body had to burn! But the same thing happened! The fire burned down and Leonhard's body was still unharmed except for a bit of singed hair and nails. And that flower—I can still see it gleaming white in his hand!

"My master ordered another fire to be kindled. But this time he commanded them to cut the body into pieces. He thought if they couldn't burn him whole, they would just burn up the pieces. But it still didn't work. By now my master was extremely agitated. He ordered them to throw the pieces of Leonhard's body into the river. Then he leaped on his horse and galloped away. No one knows where he went. He left a message of resignation as judge and disappeared.

"I was so troubled by what I had seen that I could not stay in

Scharding. The place haunted me. I wanted to get far away. I had heard that there were people like Leonhard in Moravia, so I came here to try to find them.

"My life is full of terrors. I fear the wrath of the God Leonhard served. How can I find the peace he had?

"And why didn't that flower burn? I wish I would have picked it up before they threw everything into the river! At first I thought Leonhard must have used some kind of magic, but now I know it was a sign from God. Oh, how can I find Him? Can you help me?" The man buried his face in his hands and wept.

No eyes in the room were dry as the bishop rose to his feet and stepped over to their guest. "My friend," he said softly as he laid a hand on the weeping man's shoulder, "you have come to the right place. We love and serve the same God that Leonhard Keyser did. It was God who guided your footsteps to our door. And we would love to show you the way to find true peace—the peace Leonhard died with."

CHAPTER TWELVE

"Watch the Smoke"

Ingolstadt, Germany—A.D. 1543

Martyrs Mirror page 466

Damian's weary footsteps quickened slightly when he saw the inn just ahead. *It will be so nice to rest for the night,* he thought. *It has been a long day. But so worthwhile!* His mind traveled back to the meeting he had enjoyed with his brethren that morning. It had been late afternoon by the time he had left to begin his journey back to Algau.[1]

I have been so blessed, Damian thought as he entered the inn. Taking

---

[1] This is another story in which I have built a scene around the few details the *Martyrs Mirror* gives.

a seat at a table near the window, he continued to reflect on the meeting he had attended. He was momentarily interrupted when the waiter came to take his order. "Would you like a glass of cold wine to refresh yourself while we prepare your food? We have the best in the country!"

Damian shook his head. "I do not drink wine. Please just bring me a glass of water."

The waiter looked surprised as he muttered, "I didn't think anyone would refuse a glass of our wine." Still frowning, he left with Damian's order.

Damian smiled slightly to himself as his thoughts went back to what he had heard at the meeting. *I'm sure my brothers and sisters in the tower at Zurich would be quite happy for "just" a glass of water.*

At the meeting, Brother Balthaser had shared a report of a group of twenty people—including men, women, and young girls—who had been apprehended and were confined in the "Witch Tower" in Zurich.

"The judge decreed that they will stay there in the darkness until they die," Brother Balthaser had told them. "He gave orders that they will receive only bread and water. They will never again see the light of the sun or the moon. And when prisoners die there, the dead are not taken away but are left to decay among the living."

Brother Balthaser's voice had broken before he continued, "We must pray fervently for these brothers and sisters! As our prayers reach God, He can reach down into that tower and strengthen them."

Damian's thoughts were interrupted again as the waiter returned and placed a plate of food on the table before him. "Thank you," Damian acknowledged gratefully.

As the waiter turned to leave, Damian bowed his head to give thanks for his food. An uneasy silence filled the room when Damian lifted his head. People looked at him suspiciously and some cast dark looks his way. A few heads bent together in whispered consultation.

But Damian was oblivious to this as he enjoyed his food. He didn't notice when a man slipped out the door and hurried down the street. As Damian finished the last bite of his food, he prepared to rise from the table. Suddenly the door burst open and a police officer rushed in, followed by the man who had summoned him.

Startled, Damian looked up. In a moment, he knew what had happened.

"Where's the heretic?" the officer shouted.

The other guests in the inn looked at one another uneasily. They had supported their companion in summoning the officer, but now no one wanted to betray Damian. But then the man who had summoned the officer pointed to Damian, who had just risen from the table.

Damian stepped forward as the officer approached him. "Who are you?" the officer demanded.

"My name is Damian," Damian answered respectfully.

"Where are you from?" was the next question.

"I am a resident of Algau."

"Where have you been and where are you going?"

"I was visiting friends in Ingolstadt and am returning home," Damian replied.

"Who are your friends? Why were you visiting them?"

"I cannot tell you," Damian answered firmly.

"And why not?" The officer's voice hung menacingly in the room.

"I will not betray my fellowmen."

The officer pulled a length of rope from his pocket. "We'll make you tell us," he snarled. "You're coming with me." Grasping Damian by the arm, he tied his hands together behind his back and led him out of the inn.

The officer walked rapidly toward the courthouse two blocks away, pulling Damian along. A guard saw them coming and unlocked the iron gate leading into the courtyard. The officer led Damian around to the back of the building. Pulling a ring of keys from his pocket, he fumbled single-handedly to find the correct one. Inserting it into the lock, he turned the key and opened the door.

Another guard appeared as they entered. The officer shoved Damian in his direction. "Get the jailer to lock up this scoundrel for the night. By tomorrow he'll talk. One night in that hole and he'll tell us anything we want!" The officer laughed as the guard took hold of Damian and led him away.

Minutes later Damian found himself in a tiny room—so small that if he stretched out both arms he could touch the walls on either side. In the dim light, he could faintly make out a ledge that appeared to be a bed. A bucket sat in a corner for a toilet. That was all.

He cautiously shuffled to the bed and sat down. Slowly his churning thoughts slowed, and he began to process what had happened. *So this is what prison is like.* He was grateful for the dim light that came through the grate on the door. At least the cell was not pitch dark.

Immediately he remembered the believers locked in the Witch Tower. *How must it be for them? No light. No proper food. Nothing but death to look forward to.*

Then a sobering thought engulfed him. *Is that what I'm facing? Will I be called to give my life for my faith? Or will they just lock me up and let me rot away in this prison?*

His meditations were disturbed by the sound of something moving in his cell. A creature scurried over his foot. *A rat,* Damian thought, grimacing. He pulled his feet up onto the bed and continued to sit in quiet meditation.

His thoughts became a prayer, and he prayed fervently for grace to stand firm. The long night passed with fitful sleep and many prayers as Damian interceded for himself, his fellow believers, and even his captors.

The rattle of keys told Damian the jailer was coming. *Is it morning already?* he wondered as the door to his cell opened.

"You are to appear before the judge," the jailer stated. "Come with me."

Damian followed the jailer out the same hall he had come through the night before. But instead of going outside, they went down another hall leading into a large room. As they entered the room, Damian saw the mayor, the town clerk, and the officer who had arrested him the evening before. The judge soon entered through another door and the questioning began.

"Do you confess that you are an Anabaptist?" the judge asked.

"I am," Damian answered.

"And you were in Ingolstadt to meet with more of your sect?"

"That is correct," Damian agreed.

"Where was your meeting held? Who all was present?"

"I cannot tell you."

The judge's face darkened as he glared at Damian. "You cannot tell me?"

"I will not betray my brethren," Damian answered quietly.

"Your brethren!" the judge spat out. "They are just more heretics like yourself. Are you willing to give up this heresy and be a part of the Holy Roman Church?"

"I will not deny my Lord."

"Guards, take him and make him recant," the judge ordered.

The guards sprang into action. One man grabbed a whip and began flogging Damian mercilessly. Damian fell to the floor as another guard began kicking him.

After a while, the judge motioned the guards to stop. "Are you now ready to repent of your stubbornness?" he asked Damian. "Tell me who was present at the meeting."

Although wracked with pain, Damian maintained his firm resolve. "As long as God holds my lips, I will not betray my brethren."

"Put him on the rack!" the judge commanded.

The guards bound him to the rack and began to stretch his body into unnatural lengths. Damian closed his eyes and begged God for strength to endure.

"Just give up your faith, and we will let you go free," the judge urged.

"I cannot deny my Lord," Damian repeated. "Your tortures are as nothing in light of eternity."

The judge was growing furious. "You'll wish you had repented when the fires of death creep around you."

"I do not fear your fire," Damian replied. "I fear much more the fire of hell, which will burn forever."

"Take him out of the city and burn him alive!" the judge ordered.

The guards released him from the rack. The cruelty he had endured made it impossible for Damian to walk, so the guards threw him onto a cart and took him out of the city. A crowd of townspeople followed.

Though weakened in body by the torture, Damian's faith remained strong, and he testified freely to the people who walked alongside. So convincing were his words that one man said to a companion, "This man has a faith that must either come from God or from the wicked devil. Although he appears to be a simple man, he knows much."

Another person edged closer and asked Damian, "Will you die as a true Christian?"

"Yes, I will," Damian replied.

"How will we know this?" the man persisted.

"Watch the smoke when they burn me," Damian answered. "It will ascend straight up to heaven."

When they reached the place of execution, Damian was tied to a stake and wood was piled up around him. Many eyes watched intently as the fire was lit and began to burn. The smoke ascended straight up toward heaven.[2]

"That's what he said would happen!" someone said. The crowd milled around uneasily. Was this a true Christian after all?

The executioner, seeing what was happening, asked the judge, "Have we unjustly executed this man?"

The judge tried to brush off his own

---

[2] The *Martyrs Mirror* does not say how much of a breeze was blowing, but there must have been some or it would not have been unusual.

responsibility. "You did the executing. I didn't."

"But I was only doing what you told me to do," the executioner insisted.

The judge shrugged. "That's not my worry." But inside he was shaken. Was the smoke a sign?

CHAPTER THIRTEEN

"My Happiness Comes From God"

Amsterdam, Netherlands—A.D. 1553

Martyrs Mirror page 539

Felistis looked toward the door as she heard the key turn in the lock. The door opened to reveal the jailer. "You are to report to the judge," he announced. "Come with me."

Felistis rose from the narrow stone ledge where she had been sitting and followed the jailer down the hallway. *What will I face?* she wondered. *Will this be my last day?*

She entered the courtroom behind the jailer. "Your Honor," the jailer said, bowing politely to the judge, "I have brought you the young maiden."

The judge dismissed the jailer and motioned Felistis to the end of the table where he and his councilors were seated. "What is your name?" he asked.

"I am Felistis," she replied.

"And where are you from?"

"I was born and raised in the town of Vreden," Felistis answered.

The judge shuffled the papers lying on the table before him. "I have been informed that you have attended meetings of the Anabaptists. Is this true?"

Felistis met his gaze with her honest blue eyes. "Yes, I have," she answered quietly.

"Don't you know they teach false doctrine?" he asked sternly. "And that our great emperor has decreed that everyone must attend the Holy Roman Church?"

"As far as false doctrines, I have not learned any from the Anabaptists," Felistis replied. "They adhere to the truth."

"Bah!" the judge spat out. "Truth? Their way is heresy!" He banged his fist on the table. "Where have you met with these people and who all was present?"

"I cannot tell you," Felistis replied calmly.

"Cannot tell me?" The judge's voice rose in indignation. "I have ways to make people talk."

Felistis remained unmoved.

The questions and accusations continued. "Why did you allow Anabaptists into your home? Who were they?" Throughout the whole process, Felistis remained calm, answering little or nothing.

"What shall we do with her?" the judge finally asked his advisors.

"Send her back to prison," one suggested. "Spending time in that hole will make her change her mind."

"And feed her nothing but bread and water," added another.

"Keep her in solitary confinement," came another suggestion.

"That sounds good," the judge approved. He rang a bell, and the jailer reappeared. "Take this girl back to her cell," he ordered. "Feed her nothing but bread and water and let no one talk with her."

"Yes, Your Honor," the jailer acknowledged. He beckoned Felistis to follow him.

Back in her cell, Felistis sat down on the stone ledge that also served as her bed. She spent time reflecting on her trial that morning. She rejoiced in God's grace that had helped her remain calm and not betray her brethren.

But her face sobered as she thought of her coming punishment. Turning her thoughts heavenward, she pleaded for strength to endure the trial she faced. *I've heard of others who were in solitary confinement and didn't remain faithful. Please, God, help me be faithful!*

Day after day passed and Felistis saw no one but the jailer, who faithfully brought her bread and water. She passed the lonely days by singing, praying, and reciting all the Scriptures she had memorized before she was imprisoned. Despite her deprivation, her spirit remained joyful in God.

One day Felistis was surprised to see a woman accompanying the jailer when he brought her bread and water at noon.

"My husband keeps telling me about this young girl in solitary confinement," the jailer's wife told Felistis as they stepped into the cell. "I wanted to see you for myself."

The jailer looked out into the hall as he muttered, "You aren't

supposed to talk to her. You might get me in trouble."

His wife ignored him. "Why would a young girl like you be content to sit in prison?" she asked. "How can you still be happy when you are deprived of so many things?"

"My happiness comes from God, my heavenly Father," Felistis answered. "He meets my needs even here in this lonely prison cell. He has blessed me with many things. I have a clear mind and can remember the hymns we used to sing in our worship services.

And I can recite the many Bible passages I learned before I was put in prison."

The jailer was pacing anxiously. "We need to go," he said, urging his wife to hurry. Reluctantly she followed him. At the door, she turned and cast one more puzzled look at Felistis before her husband closed and then locked the door.

In the coming weeks, the jailer's wife paid more visits to Felistis. Disregarding the judge's orders, she often spent time visiting with her, and the two became good friends.

"It's a pity one as young as you should be holed up here," she told Felistis. "I need someone to help me with my cleaning and cooking, and I have convinced my husband to let you come and help me."

Felistis looked surprised. "Are you sure it's all right? Won't your husband get in trouble if he lets me out of my cell?"

The jailer's wife didn't seem concerned. "No one ever comes into the jail except him, and they won't know you aren't here. Our house is right beside the jail, so if the judge suddenly decided he wanted to talk to you, it wouldn't take any longer to fetch you from the house than from this jail cell."

The next day the jailer led Felistis out the back door and over to his house, where his wife was waiting. "Now don't do anything foolish and get me in trouble," he growled as he left to return to the jail.

The days passed more swiftly now that Felistis had other duties to occupy her time. Although she was still a prisoner, she greatly enjoyed her increased freedom. The jailer's wife treated her almost like a sister and the two spent many hours talking while they worked.

"I admire the peace you have," the jailer's wife confessed one day. "I wish I could have it too."

"You can," Felistis urged. "You just need to repent of your sins and accept God as Lord and Savior of your life! It's worth it to know and serve the living God!" Felistis' face glowed with inner joy as she spoke of her Savior.

The jailer's wife shook her head. "It might be all right for you, but it would never work for me. My husband would lose his job and would probably end up in a prison cell instead of guarding it!"

"God will provide for you if you truly seek to serve Him," Felistis assured her. "There is no greater joy than to be one of His children."

The jailer's wife abruptly changed the subject. "I need this garbage carried out."

"Shall I take it out for you?" Felistis offered.

"Won't you run away?"

"No," Felistis replied.

Her mistress looked slightly doubtful as she started to hand the garbage to Felistis. But Felistis made no move to take it. "On second thought, I had better not do it," she said. "It would be a strong temptation for me."

After many months had passed, the judge again called for Felistis to come before him. "Have you changed your mind yet?" he questioned. "Have you given up this false religion?"

"I continue to adhere to the truth," Felistis replied firmly.

"Then we shall use other methods to make you change your mind," the judge said.

The guards led her to the torture chamber. "Just look at all these things," they taunted. "They are just waiting to tear into your body. This rack will stretch you until your arms and legs are almost pulled off. These hooks will rip the flesh from your bones."

Felistis ignored the taunts and began praying for strength to endure whatever she had to face.

The guards placed her on the rack. "Will you recant now?" the judge asked as her limbs were stretched painfully. "You will be set free if you only give up your foolish religion."

"I will not forsake my Lord," Felistis replied.

After more tormenting and questioning, the judge ordered her back to the courtroom. "Since you refuse to recant, you must die," he pronounced coldly. "In two weeks, you will meet your death by fire."

Felistis was taken back to her cell to await the execution date. The cold stone ledge felt good to her battered and bruised body.

The jailer's wife visited her cell as often as possible and tried to administer what comfort she could. "No one should have to suffer like this," she sighed as she gently rubbed the swollen limbs.

But Felistis' face still glowed with inner peace. "My God gives grace for whatever He allows," she testified. "Yes, my body is suffering great pain, but it is nothing compared to the joy of eternity with Him. Soon I will be released from this body and be with my Lord!"

On the day of the execution, the jailer's wife came to say goodbye. "I hope to meet you someday in heaven," Felistis said as she and the jailer's wife embraced before parting.

"I'll think about all you have taught me," the jailer's wife said through her tears. "You have been a true friend, and I know you are a genuine Christian."

The jailer arrived to lead Felistis to her death. "It is time to go," he said. Despite his gruff demeanor, Felistis sensed in him a reluctance to fulfill his duty. Even the tough jailer had softened toward her.

"I am ready," Felistis said. Her countenance wore the expectation of a bride waiting for her bridegroom. Her clean attire, including a white apron, seemed to be a testimony of how purely and uprightly a Christian virgin should be adorned to be acceptable before Christ.

As the fire rose around her body, Felistis' soul rose to meet her heavenly Bridegroom.

CHAPTER FOURTEEN

"My Shirt Collar... A Sign"

Bruneck, Italy—A.D. 1557-1559

Martyrs Mirror pages 560-563

Hans Brael lifted his hand in a friendly greeting as the horseback rider rode past him, but then a second rider reigned in his horse suddenly. Before Hans had time to think what was happening, the town clerk began questioning him.

"Where have you been?" he demanded.

"I have been with my brethren," Hans replied.

"Are the Anabaptists your brethren?" the clerk questioned further.

"They are," Hans admitted.

Upon hearing these words, the clerk leaped from his horse and seized Hans. Meanwhile, the first rider, who was the judge, had turned back to see what was happening. Taking Hans's girdle, he bound him tightly and made him walk like a dog alongside his horse. For several miles they plodded through the mud back to the castle in Bruneck, in the Puster Valley.

Upon reaching the castle, the judge untied Hans. Worn out from the harshness of the walk, Hans fell to the ground, unable to stand.

"Why did you tie him so tightly and make him walk like that?" the castle lord scolded the judge. "He might be a heretic, but you don't need to kill him before he has a trial!"

The castle guards searched Hans thoroughly and confiscated all his belongings, then cast him into prison.

The next day he was brought before the lord of the castle. "So you have joined yourself to the Anabaptists?" the lord asked. "Those who are enemies of the holy church of God?"

"I am a Christian and part of the true church of God," Hans replied.

"What do you believe about infant baptism?"

"As the Scriptures say, I believe he that believes and is baptized shall be saved. An infant cannot believe and therefore has no need of baptism."

"And what is your view of the sacrament?" the lord asked.

"The bread and wine of the Communion table are but symbols of Christ's sacrifice on the cross. The bread symbolizes His body—beaten and bruised for our sins. The wine represents His shed blood, which redeems all who call upon Him." Hans spoke clearly and sincerely.

"You are in error," the lord told him. "We all know that Christ said to His followers when He instituted Communion that, 'This is my body' and 'This is my blood.'"

"But how could Christ give His actual body and blood when He was right there present with them?" Hans countered.

The lord refused to answer the question, instead urging Hans to recant of his heresy.

"I will not give up my faith," Hans answered firmly. "I serve the Lord Jesus Christ and follow the truth as He taught in the Scriptures. I will not turn back."

"Take him back to prison!" the lord ordered.

Eight days later, they brought Hans forth from prison again, and the lord and six others examined him. But Hans remained as firm in his faith as before.

After another eight days, Hans was brought before the entire council—this time to be examined by the judge. "Your faith is a delusion; your church is a sect," the judge declared.

"It is neither a sect nor a delusion; it is the church of God," Hans replied.

"It is the devil's church, so how could it be the church of God?" the judge retorted angrily. He glared at Hans.

"It is the true church of God," Hans responded boldly.

The judge hurled more questions at him: "Who are your brethren? Where did you stay when you came to the city? Who served your meals?"

"God's children do not share information that would be detrimental to each other. If you ask me about my faith, I will tell you. But of the names and locations of my brethren, I will not speak."

"We will torture you severely if you do not tell us," the judge threatened.

Hans looked around the table at the men sitting there. "Do any of you think it would be right to betray those who have shown kindness to me?"

The council members looked at one another. "We would not consider it right if someone did that to us," one of them finally admitted.

But the judge became even angrier. "Are you charging this honorable council with making unfair demands?" he shouted. "Just tell us what we want to know, or we will deal very harshly with you."

When Hans remained silent, they sent him back to prison. The next time he was brought out, they took him straight to the rack and began torturing him. Hans endured the torture so patiently that the bystanders could not keep from weeping.

The executioner then tied a rope to Hans's hands and suspended him in midair as the judge continued to admonish him to spare himself of all this pain. "Just tell us what we want to know," the judge demanded.

"I will betray no one," Hans replied bravely. "I will rather endure whatever misery God permits you to place on me."

The executioner then tied a large stone to Hans's feet so its weight would inflict even more pain.

"You people swear to each other that you won't betray one another," the judge said angrily when he saw he could get no information from Hans.

"We do not swear about anything," Hans replied. "We don't betray each other because that would be wrong."

The judge and his council then left the torture chamber with Hans still hanging from the rope. The executioner, who was still present, again urged him to answer their questions. "If you don't, we will torment you until we have pulled your limbs from your body."

"I will endure whatever is laid upon me," Hans replied. "You can do no more than God permits."

"Do you really think God looks down and sees what we are doing?" the executioner asked. "That is a ridiculous idea."

Just then the council returned. "The lady of the castle requests that we torment him no more but send him back to prison."

Later the lord and some priests questioned Hans for two days in a row, but they could accomplish nothing. He remained steadfast.

Three days later they put him in a deep, dark, filthy dungeon at the base of a tower. It was so dark that the only way he knew when nighttime came was when the air became a little cooler. As time went on, the dampness of the cell rotted the clothes off his body. He wrapped himself in a coarse blanket they had given him. The only part of his clothes he had left was the collar of his shirt, which he hung on the wall.

Whenever he was taken out of the tower for questioning, the stench that clung to him was so bad that no one could stand it for any length of time.

"I have never smelled such a horrible stench," one councilor said.

Because the light hurt his eyes, Hans was glad when the questioning was over and he could return to the tower.

"My Shirt Collar...A Sign"

The tower contained many small animals and reptiles. These terrified Hans for a time until he got used to them. When his food was let down to him, he had to eat it right away so the rats and mice wouldn't get it. This was not hard to do as he was nearly starving. Sometimes mice got into his water pitcher and drowned. One day Hans found a large stone and placed it on top of the pitcher so the mice couldn't enter.

His worst affliction, however, was the isolation from his brethren. One church brother was able to get word to him that if he was still faithful to God, he should send some token to them, even if it was only a piece of straw.

There is not even a piece of straw in this place, Hans lamented. Suddenly he remembered. *My shirt collar! I can send that to them as a sign that I am still faithful to God.*

Hans's brethren gladly received his token of faithfulness. But their hearts were filled with compassion when they realized the extreme poverty and misery he was enduring. They sent a message back to him: "We will try to send you clothes or whatever you need."

Hans received their message gratefully, but he refused the offer. "If I received gifts from you, they would torture me to try to find out who sent them. The garment of patience must clothe me."

Hans lay in the tower all summer. That fall they moved him to another prison. For thirty-seven weeks, Hans had to stand with one hand and one foot in stocks while the guards and others ridiculed him. "Look, here is a holy man; nobody is as wise as he is. There he stands as a light to the world and a witness of the people of God and His church." The words, though mostly true, were said in a mocking tone, deriding Hans's faith in God.

Although he could not communicate with the church brethren, God had other means of encouraging him—such as the time a nobleman told him to be courageous. "You know you have the truth on your side. Your faith is the true faith."

One day Hans, still in stocks, sent for the clerk who had captured him. The clerk came quickly and asked what he wanted. "You are the reason I am in prison," Hans told him. "But I never did you any wrong."

The clerk didn't know what to say. "I had to do it," he finally stammered.

"But God sees what you have done, and He will judge you for it," Hans said.

The clerk was so dumbfounded at Hans's words that he couldn't reply. Frightened, he left the cell.

One morning a few weeks later, one of the servants of the castle came to Hans. "The clerk died last night," he reported. "It was very strange. He was alive and well, but then he was suddenly seized with great fear. He cried and moaned terribly for about fifteen minutes, saying he had done wrong. Then he was gone. The lord and his lady are terrified."

Sometime later the lord of the castle also died suddenly, creating more fear. The lord's wife sent word to Hans that she would have him released if he would but recant. "She says she will take upon herself any sins you commit by recanting so you will not be guilty," the servant reported.

"She has enough sins of her own," Hans replied. "Let her repent of those. She does not need mine."

Slowly another winter passed. Finally the court decided Hans should be sent to sea. "There you will have to do as they say, or you will be stripped and scourged. This is what happens to evildoers like you."

"I will trust in the Lord, who is on the sea as well as on the land," Hans replied. "God will give me grace and patience to endure."

He was let out of prison to walk about the castle for two days so he could learn to walk again. He had been bound for nearly two years and had not seen the sun for about a year and a half.

Hans exhorted everyone in the castle to repentance before he left. He even challenged the lady of the castle to repent. "Don't do harm to godly people," he admonished. "They aren't hurting you in any way."

The lady was moved to tears as Hans spoke. "Never again will I lay hands upon innocent people," she promised. She gave Hans some money for his journey and dismissed him.

The servant with whom Hans was to travel to the sea was a wicked man. At every opportunity, he called Hans a rogue or some other derogatory term, but Hans meekly bore the taunts, relying on God's grace to help him endure.

For two days they traveled until they reached the town of Niederdorf. At the tavern where they stopped to sleep, the servant became so drunk with wine that he fell asleep on one of the tables and rolled off. Hans escaped out the front door and fled across the countryside. After an arduous journey, he finally returned to his brethren in Austria.

Hans later received word of the death of the servant who had been taking him to sea. The judge who had so wrongly treated him at his arrest and trial also died a very miserable death about two years later.

Hans continued to serve God faithfully, encouraging others to cling to the Lord with a true heart and to claim His strength and patience in suffering.

Chapter Fifteen

"Why Have You Betrayed Me?"

Leeuwarden, Netherlands—A.D. 1558-1559

Martyrs Mirror pages 591-611

"Mr. Jacques! Is it really you?" The well-dressed gentleman smiled as he called out a greeting to the peddler. "I have long been wanting to find you and talk with you again!"

Mr. Jacques extended his hand. "Greetings, Mr. de Wael! It has indeed been many years since we last spoke." The two men fell into friendly conversation.

At last Mr. de Wael said regretfully, "It has been a pleasure to speak with you again, but I must continue on my other errands. But do come by my house and pick up the letter I have there for you. Had I known I would meet you today, I would have brought it with me."

"I will stop by on my return home," Jacques promised.

That evening Jacques stopped his carriage at the hitching post in front of a well-kept house and yard. His quick eyes took in the perfectly trimmed grass and carefully pruned bushes. The stone house stood boldly in the center of the estate while an iron fence marched around the perimeter of the yard. A servant appeared at the gate and ushered Jacques into the yard.

"Welcome, my friend." Mr. de Wael greeted him warmly, handing him the letter. "Step inside and be refreshed. It would be an honor to have you as my guest."

Jacques shook his head regretfully. "I would indeed be honored to stay for a while, but I promised my wife I would try to be home this evening. I must continue on my way as soon as possible."

Mr. de Wael seemed genuinely disappointed that Jacques could not remain with him, but he responded kindly. "Ah, yes, your wife and family need you too. But do come again when your wagon is full of wares. I should like to do business with you. When can you come?"

"I plan to pass through here again in two weeks," Jacques replied. "I shall be happy to accept your invitation then."

"Good. I shall look for you," Mr. de Wael said.

As Jacques continued home, he thought about Mr. de Wael. *It's surprising that he took such an interest in me. Why is he so eager to do business with me, a poor peddler? He could buy from anyone he wants!*

But Jacques was a man with a simple faith, and he spent little time analyzing why a rich man might choose to do business with a poor man. *I'm just glad he wants to buy my wares,* he concluded.

Meanwhile, back at Mr. de Wael's house, a trap was being set. Mr. de Wael hastened to his writing desk and prepared a message to send to the council at Leeuwarden.

> Dear Sirs:
> I have among my acquaintances a man by the name of Jacques d'Auchy, a peddler by trade. He is, I am told, part of the sect of heretics called Anabaptists. I have arranged for him to come to my home on business in one fortnight from when I am writing this message. Please send a commissary and a bailiff at the appointed time that we may apprehend this man.
> Yours truly,
> Mr. de Wael, Councilor of Harlingen

When the time came for Jacques to return to Mr. de Wael, all was prepared. Jacques once again stopped at the hitching post. This time his carriage overflowed with goods he was hoping to sell.

Mr. de Wael, seeing Jacques arrive, sent a messenger to fetch the bailiff while he went out to meet the peddler. "Ah, my friend, how good to see you! How are your wife and family?"

After the greetings were exchanged, Mr. de Wael turned his attention to the loaded carriage. "And what valuable wares have you brought to sell today?"

As the two men looked at the merchandise, another horse and carriage clattered in the lane. One of the occupants leaped off the carriage and came over to the two men. Immediately Mr. de Wael's friendly demeanor changed to one of disgust and malice. "Apprehend him!" he said. "This is the man."

The bailiff seized Jacques. "Hold still," he said gruffly, searching

him for anything he might be trying to hide.

Jacques, recovering from his initial shock, turned toward Mr. de Wael. "Oh, my lord, what have you done? Why have you betrayed me? Why do you seek my life?" Jacques' words were full of sorrow and reproach.

"Just allow yourself to be arrested," Mr. de Wael snarled. "I had to do this to keep my oath." He pulled a paper from his pocket and read in a cruel voice the mandate he was obeying. "Now, I must ask you about four other men of your kind. Tell us where they are."

"I will not betray or deceive anyone," Jacques replied. "If you have heard any complaints about me, please tell me."

"I have not heard any complaints about you," Mr. de Wael admitted. "You are not being apprehended because of a crime but because you adhere to heresy. You are one of the Anabaptists, right?"

"I have not adhered to any heresy," Jacques responded. "Nor do I consider myself an Anabaptist, for according to God's Word I have received but one baptism upon the confession of my faith."

"What do you believe about the Roman Catholic Church?" Mr. de Wael asked.

"It is not of God," Jacques answered promptly.

Mr. de Wael's face immediately bore a look of great sorrow, and he sighed deeply. "Oh, Jacques, must you fall into my hands?"

"My lord," Jacques replied, "I trusted you because we have known each other for years. I will gladly and from my heart forgive you for this. It is my earnest desire that the Lord may have mercy upon you."

"You are very kind to bestow such a favor on me," Mr. de Wael said somewhat sarcastically. "But I do not believe I have done wrong before God. I am only keeping my oath, which God commands us to do."

"Do you think this is right before God and man? The time will come when you will find out otherwise." Jacques spoke with conviction.

Mr. de Wael ignored Jacques' words and dismissed him, saying, "You will be examined at Leeuwarden concerning your faith and doctrine."

Once he was in prison, Jacques' wife came to visit him. "The jailer refused to let me in at first," she told him. "But after bystanders took pity on me and implored him, he finally agreed to let me in for a while."

Jacques looked anxiously at his wife, who was heavy with child. "Oh, my beloved, go home and comfort yourself in the Lord, for I am imprisoned here for the Word of God. I have injured no one."

"May the Lord strengthen you in the truth," his wife replied. "There will be an eternal crown for you. Oh, I wish I could die too and inherit that blissful life with you! That would make me so happy!" His wife's words were filled with longing.

"Do not be grieved if I have to go before you do," Jacques comforted her. "It is the Lord's will."

By now the jailer had returned and was listening to their exchange. "Be gone—quick!" he demanded to Jacques' wife.

Jacques spoke up. "Please let us alone with God for a little while," he begged.

The jailer refused. "Go, I said." He shoved Jacques' wife out the door ahead of him. And Jacques was alone once again.

Ten weeks later, the jailer came to him one afternoon. "You are to appear before the commissary to be examined for your faith. Come with me." Joyfully Jacques accompanied the jailer, glad to be able to testify for his Lord.

After greeting him, the commissary said, "Jacques, I have been commissioned by the king to examine you in regards to your faith."

"Well, my lord," Jacques responded, "let it be done then in the name of the Lord."

After conversing for some time concerning the faith, the commissary asked Jacques about his early life, where he was born, where he lived, what his life was like as a youth, and on up to the present day. After the questioning, Jacques was led back to prison.

The next afternoon he was again summoned before the commissary. Immediately the commissary began to revile and blaspheme the pastors and the flock of Christ. "Isn't it a pity that people are so deceived?"

"It certainly is," Jacques replied.

The commissary glared at him for a moment. "I'm talking about you and others who forsake the holy church and allow yourselves to be deceived by mischievous idlers and vagabonds."

"I have not been deceived by any such," Jacques replied calmly.

"Are you not deceived when you believe such beggars as Menno Simons, Hendrik van Vreden, and other rascals?"

"These men have not deceived us but have taught the Word of God. The Lord will judge all things well."

"I know you people," the commissary said. "If you could, you would kill us all, just like the people in Münster tried to do."

"My lord," Jacques begged, "do not speak that way. You know us better than that. You have been on the council here for twenty years, and you know we would never try to kill you."

"Then where does all this uproar and mutiny come from?" the commissary demanded.

"Those things are from the devil," Jacques declared. "We have nothing to do with those in Münster—or any others who try to use force."

After a time of discussion, the commissary began to calm down a bit. "You must allow yourself to be instructed by those more learned and wiser than you," he told Jacques.

Following this exchange, Jacques was returned to his prison cell for several days. Then he was brought back to the same room to be questioned by another inquisitor. "Jacques," he said, "I am very glad of one thing. I'm told you will confess your guilt if it can be proved by the Scriptures that you have transgressed the commandments of God. Do you still agree to this?"

"I am ready to listen to all good instruction from the Word of God," Jacques replied.

The inquisitor first questioned Jacques about his baptism, disputing long on the validity of infant baptism, which Jacques repeatedly told him was not taught in the Scriptures. Finally the inquisitor ended the interview. "Farewell, Jacques," he said. "Consider the matter well and pray diligently to God about it. Your time is short."

The inquisitor was right in that Jacques' time was short, but it was not in the way he supposed.

One night not long after this, while most of the world slept, a man crept through the corridor of the prison to Jacques' cell. When he left again, Jacques' earthly life, so faithfully lived for God, had ended.[1]

Mr. de Wael, true to Jacques' earlier words, found out just how wrong he had been in betraying the peddler. The common people of Leeuwarden hated him for his treachery. And then God smote him with leprosy, which caused many taunts from his enemies. To save his life, Mr. de Wael hired a boatman to take him from Leeuwarden.

The people followed, hurling insults and stones at the disgraced man. "Judas! Traitor!" they screamed. "You're a rogue!"

The boatman rowed hard as the stones continued to fly. "Please spare my life!" he cried. "I am just following orders!"

Although he escaped the stones, Mr. de Wael spent the rest of his life wandering from place to place. He was despised and scorned by men until the leprosy finally took his life.

---

[1] The *Martyrs Mirror* does not tell us who murdered Jacques.

CHAPTER SIXTEEN

"My Blood Will Be Seen in the Sun"

Warthausen, Germany—A.D. 1571

Martyrs Mirror pages 893-894

"Tell us about your religion," the neighbors begged Hans. "Read to us from your copy of the Word of God."

Hans Misel, a weaver by trade, willingly complied with their request. He loved the Lord and delighted in sharing the good news of salvation with others.

The neighbors listened intently as Hans shared the simple truths of the Bible with them. "The Bible is free to all," he told them. "God wants you to read it and learn for yourselves how He wants you to live."

"But I thought only the priests can understand the Bible," one man ventured.

"That's what the priests want you to think," Hans told them. "But God's Word is plain and simple; even the common man can read it and understand it."

Suddenly the meeting was interrupted. The clerk from the castle had arrived, along with a number of servants. "It is not legal for you to teach others about your false God," the clerk announced. He drew his sword and struck Hans on the chest with the hilt.

The neighbors who had begged Hans to teach them backed away fearfully.

"Your way is heresy," the clerk sneered, striking Hans again. "I could do more than this to you."

Hans remained calm and quiet, but his silence only seemed to infuriate the clerk. Drawing back his arm, he struck Hans again, this time with the blade of his sword. "I could kill you!" he screamed.

But Hans was not afraid. "Calm yourself," he said to the clerk. "It is not good for you to get so worked up."

The neighbors drew near again, feeling emboldened by Hans's calm response. "Let this man alone!" they cried. "He has done no wrong."

The clerk glared at the people. "How dare you contradict my words!" He swung his sword threateningly toward the crowd. Without any further words, the clerk bound Hans, and he and the servants led him away to a house close to the castle.

All night they reveled, making fun of Hans and treating him very unkindly. "Here," one man said, handing him a Latin Bible. "If you like to read the Bible so well, read this to us." Hans, unable to read Latin, refused the book and remained silent.

"This man thinks he's so good he can teach others, but he can't even read the Bible!" they mocked.

The next day they took him to the castle and put him in a tower. Many priests came to see him. "Give up your heresy," they urged. "Save your soul from hell."

"My soul has been saved by the blood of Jesus," Hans replied. "As God says in His Word, 'The blood of Jesus Christ his Son cleanseth us from all sin.'"[1]

The priests glared at Hans. "You are but a young man. Why do you think you can teach us the Scriptures? We are the ones who understand God's Word. You are but an ignorant weaver and have not been taught the Word of God."

"You teach people heresy," Hans declared. "In His Word, God tells us, 'For there is one God, and one mediator between God and men, the man Christ Jesus.'[2] You take the Word of God and make it say what you want it to say. God's Word is plain and simple, and the common person can understand it. I beg you to consider your ways and bow before God before it is too late."

The priests shifted uneasily. This was not going well. The young man before them knew his Bible thoroughly and could refute everything they said. They moved away and conversed in low tones for a bit. "We'll see if you still maintain your stubborn ways once the executioner tries you," one of them sneered as they left the tower.

The next day the executioner led Hans from his cell to the torture chamber. "If you do not wish to feel the pain from these instruments,

---

[1] 1 John 1:7

[2] 1 Timothy 2:5

you need but recant of your heretical ways," the executioner told him.

"You may do to my body what you will," Hans replied. "But I will not give up my faith in God."

Without further words, the executioner and his men seized Hans and laid him on the rack, fastening his limbs firmly. Then they began stretching his body.

"Are you ready to recant now?" the executioner asked when Hans's body was stretched to the utmost.

"I will not give up my faith in God," Hans repeated.

"Bring the whip," the executioner ordered. Lash after lash soon cut into Hans's already tortured body.

Hans maintained his steadfast commitment to God despite the intensity of the pain inflicted on him. At last the executioner and his men ceased torturing him and carried him back to the tower.

"We can do nothing with this man," they reported to the lady of the castle.

The lady looked troubled. "Fetch me the priests. I don't know how to deal with him either."

The priests gladly answered her summons, and the lady of the castle implored them for help. "What shall we do with this man who refuses to return to the church of God?" she asked. "I don't know how to deal with him."

"The imperial law states that such dissenters shall be put to death," one of the priests replied.

The lady of the castle accepted their advice. She called together her council and presented them with the verdict. "The law requires that such a man be put to death," she told them.

Several council members refused to support the sentence, but the voices of the rest prevailed and Hans was sentenced to die a week later.

The night before his execution, some of his friends tried to help him escape by digging a hole next to the tower. Closer and closer to Hans they came. When Hans heard them, he begged them to stop. "I will not try to escape," he told them.

The next morning someone offered him some food before he was taken to the place of execution, but Hans refused to eat. "Please leave me in peace for a little while," he entreated.

Although surprised by the strange request, the executioner granted it.

Hans went into a corner, lifted his hands to heaven, and began to pray. "God, I thank you that you have brought me to this hour and have found me worthy to suffer for you. Give me strength and courage that I might die the death of the upright. I thank you for all the benefits you have shown to me, and I beseech you to help me now in my last hour. Father, into your hands I commend my spirit."

The executioner, quietly observing Hans, muttered, "This man is bolder than all the rest of us."

When Hans had finished his prayer, he got to his feet with a smile. He was ready to die. A priest went with him to the place of execution, imploring him to turn from his heresy.

"My soul is safe with God," Hans said confidently. "But you need to repent of your whoredom, your villainy, and your idolatrous, ungodly life. May God have mercy on your soul."

Before beheading him, the executioner again tried to make Hans recant. "It's not too late. I have the authority to set you free if you repent."

But Hans refused. "I will seal my faith with my blood," he said. "And after I die, my blood will be seen in the sun."

The executioner, seeing that Hans would not change his mind, raised his sword and struck off his head.

But then a strange thing happened. Hans's decapitated body remained standing, with his hands uplifted as though in prayer. The executioner had to push the body over.

Hans's body was cut into pieces so it could be burned more quickly. But then another miracle occurred—his head and hair would not burn! It was removed from the ashes, unscathed, and was buried.

Three days later, at noon, the sun became blood-red in appearance. Puzzled villagers gathered in the streets and discussed the strange phenomenon. "What is going on?" they asked each other in alarm. "The sun looks like it's covered with blood! Is this the end of the world?"

Questions flew back and forth as the villagers milled about. Suddenly one man exclaimed, "Remember that heretic who was killed three days ago? He said his blood would be seen in the sun!"

The crowd fell silent. What kind of man had been killed? Was he maybe not a heretic after all?

CHAPTER SEVENTEEN

"I Never Slept Better"

Breda, Netherlands—A.D. 1572

Martyrs Mirror pages 929-931

Geleyn looked up from the shoe he was stitching as the door to his shop opened. "Good morning, brother!" he said, greeting the young man who had entered.[1] Geleyn knew him well; he was an apprentice at Pieter de Gulicker's tailor shop.

"Greetings!" the young man said. "Brother Jan sent me with a message." He glanced around the shop as though looking for someone.

---

[1] The beginning of this story is an imaginary scene to give a prelude to the main events described in the *Martyrs Mirror*.

"We are alone," Geleyn assured him, guessing the nature of the message.

The youth smiled slightly, but he still kept his voice low when he spoke. "A meeting is planned for tomorrow night at ten o'clock at Pieter's home." He paused as his eyes brightened. "There is going to be a wedding!"

Geleyn smiled. "Ah, a special meeting! If God so wills, I will be there. Thank you for bringing the message. Give my greetings to Brother Pieter and Brother Jan."

The young apprentice left the shop and Geleyn returned to his work. A smile played on his lips as he thought of the upcoming meeting and the planned wedding. *We have been blessed,* he reflected. *God has given us relative peace here in our area. Our church has even grown because of those who fled here from areas of persecution.*

The next evening Geleyn made his way cautiously to Pieter de Gulicker's home, where he joined the others who had gathered. *There must be nearly a hundred brothers and sisters here!* he observed as he looked over the group.

That same evening, the town bailiff and his steward were sitting in a local house drinking wine and other strong drink. They looked up when a man entered the house. "I have received word that the Christians are gathering tonight at the house of Pieter de Gulicker," he said.

"What?" The bailiff leaped to his feet, knocking over his glass of wine. "We'll disturb that nest and exterminate the whole band at once! Come!" He motioned to his steward, and they left the house.

The two men quickly assembled their servants, and the group stealthily approached the house where Pieter lived. "We'll get the whole group at once! Won't this be fun!" The bailiff chuckled at the thought.

But all was quiet when they reached the house. "There doesn't seem to be anything happening," the bailiff muttered to his steward, obviously disappointed.

"It is still early. Maybe the meeting is later—after dark," the steward suggested. "The messenger didn't say when they were gathering. These Christians are sly. They gather when we least expect them to."

"We'll come back," the bailiff vowed. Quietly they slipped away.

Half an hour later, they again approached the house. As before, all was quiet. "That man must have lied to me," the bailiff sputtered angrily.

"It is not even ten o'clock yet," the steward said. "There is still time. Let's check back in another hour. I'll send one of my servants, and he can report back to us."

True to his word, the steward sent a servant about an hour later to see if the Christians had assembled for their meeting. The excited servant soon returned. "There must be a hundred of them there!" he exclaimed.

"Let's go!" the bailiff ordered.

For the third time, the group of armed men moved stealthily down the street. Cautiously they approached the door of the house.

—◆—

Geleyn drank in the words as Brother Jan preached earnestly to the group. Suddenly the door burst open and the bailiff and his men rushed into the room, brandishing swords, pistols, and other weapons. Before Geleyn had time to react, one of the men grabbed his arm and pulled him to his feet.

"You people are heretics!" the bailiff screamed. "You are enemies of the true church of God! We'll arrest every one of you!"

Held tightly, Geleyn heard the cries of alarm as his fellow Christians tried to escape. The bailiff's men soon returned from other parts of the house where they had captured some of the others.

"Well, we caught a few of them," the bailiff muttered angrily. "But we should have caught the whole nest!"

"These creatures are as slippery as eels!" another man exclaimed. "Just when you think you have them cornered up, they vanish."

"They're demonic," another man said. "Only demons could disappear like that."

Geleyn glanced around, trying to figure out who else had been captured. He saw Brother Pieter, Brother Arent, Brother Cornelis, and the young apprentice who had brought him word of the meeting. And was that Brother Jan over there? Geleyn also heard a comment about some women, but he couldn't see who they were.

The men herded the prisoners out the door and down the street. Nobody spoke. The *tramp, tramp, tramp* of their footsteps echoed through

Faithful Unto Death

the silence. Their steps seemed to be saying *caught, caught, caught.*

Before long the group arrived at the house where the men had been drinking. Geleyn caught a glimpse of three women being ushered into another room, but his attention quickly returned to his own plight as the rattle of chains and the clank of iron sounded nearby.

Soon Geleyn and his fellow brethren were securely fastened to the wall of the room. There was little space to move around, with both ankles securely locked in irons and chained together. Another chain fastened the ankle chain to the wall.

The brethren did not speak much through the night. Each seemed lost in his own thoughts. Geleyn's mind struggled to grasp the grim reality of the situation. *What will happen to my wife and children? Who will provide for them?*

But my God shall supply all your needs… The comforting words flashed into Geleyn's mind. *Of course. God will take care of them.* He bowed his head and spent the rest of the night interceding for his wife, his children, his church, his fellow prisoners, and his captors. He also prayed for himself that he would remain strong in his faith.

When morning arrived, it brought with it a surprise visitor. Brother Cornelis' uncle Michael came to visit and encourage the prisoners. "The sisters who were captured last evening escaped during the night," he told them. "They told us where you were."

His presence cheered the imprisoned brethren, and they sang and prayed together. "Be strong in the faith," he exhorted them.

Before Michael departed, however, a less welcome visitor arrived. It was the bailiff himself. "Well, who do we have here?" he sneered when he saw Michael. "Another heretic? You also belong to these people, so you must stay here with them!"

He turned to his men, who had arrived just behind him. "Chain him up!"

The day passed slowly. The bailiff and town clerk meticulously recorded information about each prisoner—who he was, where he was from, what his occupation was, and so on.

"All their possessions belong to us now," the bailiff said when the lists were complete. He looked at his men. "Go claim everything for the town."

The prisoners stared at the bailiff in shocked silence. Then Brother Pieter ventured bravely, "What about our families?"

The bailiff turned his smirking gaze to rest on Pieter. "I don't care one bit about your families. They can starve." His cold, hard words cut to the heart of each prisoner. Slowly he allowed his gaze to pass from one man to the next, seeming to relish in the agony he saw on their faces. "You heretics deserve nothing!" he hissed. Turning around, he left the room.

"Let's pray." Brother Michael's voice finally broke the silence after the bailiff had left. Fervent prayers ascended as the brethren pleaded with God to care for their families. They did not know how He would answer, but they committed their loved ones into His keeping.

The next day the prisoners were led out of the house and taken to the larger town of Breda to be questioned about their beliefs.

A schoolmaster accompanied the group. "These people are so stubborn and contrary in what they believe," he said bitterly to the bailiff's steward as they walked along. "I don't know why they can't just be like the rest of us instead of trying to be different."

The steward nodded. "It would make our lives a lot easier," he said. "Then we wouldn't be transporting prisoners in this August heat!"

"I must say, though," the schoolmaster continued grudgingly, "they live more honorable lives than most people. They teach their children the fear of God and use discipline when needed. Their children are my best students in school. Even though I despise their religion, I don't like to see them suffer like this. Why, their wives and children were driven away from their homes with nothing! That's not right!"

The group entered the town of Breda and proceeded to the courthouse. Here the captive men were subjected to a barrage of questions, promises, and threats.

"Who were the others at your meeting? Where do they live? Who is your leader? Tell us what we want to know, and we will return your belongings and let you go free. You can be with your families again. But if you don't give up your faith, we will torture you!" Relentlessly the bailiff and the judge grilled the men, repeating the same questions and threats over and over.

"Give these men a taste of the whip," the judge ordered when no one budged from his faith.

Geleyn closed his eyes and prayed for strength as blow after blow fell across his back.

"Stop!" a voice cried out. "I have had enough. I renounce my Christianity. I will tell you whatever you want."

Geleyn opened his eyes and saw the captors releasing the leg irons on Pieter's ankles. *Oh, Pieter,* he mourned silently, *how could you turn your back on your faith? May God have mercy on you!*

As Pieter was led away, Geleyn heard the judge order the executioner to follow him. "Behead him outside the city. He's a coward."

Geleyn forgot his grief over his friend's failure as his own trials continued. He lost track of time as they continued to torture him to make him give up his faith. By now most of the other prisoners had been taken to a prison cell.

"Who else was at your meeting? Who is your leader? Why don't you baptize your babies?" Following his Lord's example, Geleyn remained silent as the questions flew at him.

"We'll make him talk," declared one of the duke's men, who had come to Breda for the trials. "Let's string him up by his thumb."

While the duke's men stripped off Geleyn's clothes, the executioner grabbed a stout rope that was attached to a pulley and fastened it securely around Geleyn's right thumb. Then the men tugged and pulled until his feet left the floor. They continued pulling until his body hung suspended in midair, then they secured the rope around a post.

The executioner looked around the room. Spying a weight sitting in a corner, he lugged it over to Geleyn. Using another piece of rope, he hung the weight from Geleyn's left foot to inflict even more pain and agony to his already tortured body.

Grabbing a torch, the executioner burned the flesh under Geleyn's arms. Then the duke's men picked up whips and flogged him. Geleyn's body was beaten back and forth until it seemed his thumb would surely be torn off.

At last the men grew tired of their sport and sat down at a nearby table to play cards. An hour passed, with Geleyn forgotten while they engaged in their idle play. When their game was over, one of the men told the executioner, "Question him again. Maybe now he will tell us something."

The executioner went over to Geleyn's silent body. "The man is dead!" he exclaimed, gazing at the still form.

"He can't be," one of the duke's men replied. He darted over and grabbed Geleyn's free arm and began yanking it roughly, as if to pull it off. After a few minutes, they began to see signs of life. The executioner removed the weight from Geleyn's foot and untied the rope that suspended him.

Then the questioning began again. But Geleyn continued steadfast, refusing to share any information that would bring harm to his brethren.

"Burn him alive!" the judge ordered. "That's all these heretics are good for."

Almost too weak to walk, Geleyn was led away to a prison cell to await his execution. He was overjoyed when he discovered himself in the same cell as Jan and the young apprentice. They too had been sentenced to be burned.

The three men shared their experiences, rejoicing that they were counted worthy to suffer for Christ.

"I felt no pain while I was suspended by my thumb," Geleyn testified. "It was as though I was in a deep sleep. I never slept better in my own bed than I did while hanging in the torture chamber."

When the day of the execution dawned, the three men were led to the stakes that had been prepared. Fires were lit, and the flames leaped around the bound men. Contrary to nature, the flames leaping around Geleyn were wafted away from his body as though an unseen force was directing them.

The executioner frowned. What was going on? He picked up a long fork and thrust Geleyn's body into the flames, holding it there until life had fled.

Geleyn's sufferings were finally over.

CHAPTER EIGHTEEN

"I Have Nothing Else"

Delft, Netherlands—A.D. 1570-1572

Martyrs Mirror pages 931-944

Jan Hendrickss drew his boat up to the dock and tied it fast. He breathed a contented sigh as he picked up his knapsack and a bucket of fish and stepped onto the shore. *God blessed me with a good run of herring today,* he rejoiced. *Now homeward!* His steps quickened at the thought of his loved ones waiting for him.[1]

Lisbeth will have supper ready, he thought, anticipating the meal and

---

[1] The first part has more fictional details than usual to lead to the *Martyrs Mirror* account.

the relaxing evening to come. Soon he reached the gate of his home.

"Papa! Papa!" Jan's musings were interrupted by the joyful cry of his little son running toward him as fast as his sturdy little legs could carry him. "Papa! You're home!" Heyndricks flung his arms around his beloved papa's legs.

Setting down his knapsack and bucket, Jan swung Heyndricks up onto his shoulders. "Soon you'll be too big to ride on my shoulders," he told him. "You're growing up!" He picked up the knapsack and bucket with one hand, then clasped Heyndricks' feet with the other and walked toward the house.

"Look! Mama and Baby are waiting for us at the door," Jan said. He swung Heyndricks to the ground as they reached the house. He greeted his wife and took the baby from her arms.

The evening passed pleasantly. Once the children were tucked in bed, Jan spoke softly to Lisbeth. "I'm hearing word that King Charles is cracking down on the Christians. There are reports of arrests and imprisonments. Our turn may be coming, my dearest."

Lisbeth clasped her hands together, and her eyes filled with tears. "Oh, Jan!" she whispered. "Do be careful! What would we do without you?"

Jan reached for his Bible. "The answers are all here, Lisbeth," he reminded her. Late into the night, the couple read and prayed and talked, finding courage to face the unknown.

―――― ◆ ――――

Jan looked up from the letter he was writing when he heard the key in the lock. The jailer swung open the door of the prisoners' cell. "Jan, come with me," he ordered gruffly.

Bewildered, Jan laid down his pen and paper and rose to his feet. "Where are we going?" he asked.

"Downstairs."

Jan's mind whirled as he followed the jailer down the steps. *I've been in prison for nearly a year, and not once have they taken me from our cell. What do they want with me now?*

The jailer led him to the sheriff's hall, where Jan saw a group of men assembled—the bailiff, the judges, and the burgomasters.

"Good day, gentlemen," Jan greeted politely.

The men returned the greeting, then the bailiff directed Jan to a bench and told him to be seated.

"How old are you?" the bailiff asked.

"I don't know exactly," Jan replied. "About twenty-eight."

"Where were you born?"

"At Swartawael," Jan answered.

"And how long have you lived in Delft?"

"Five years, if you count the time I have been confined here."

"Why haven't you baptized your children?"

"I have never read in the Bible that we should baptize children," Jan said.

"The Bible talks about whole households being baptized," the bailiff replied.

"That is true," Jan agreed. "But it also says they all rejoiced when they believed in the Lord. Infants cannot do that."

The clerk spoke up next. "Where does the Bible forbid us to baptize infants?"

Jan returned a question about a common gambling practice. "Does the Bible forbid throwing dice?"

"We know it's forbidden," the clerk answered. "But I cannot prove it to you from the Bible."

"You're right, it is nowhere forbidden," Jan agreed. "Yet we all know it is an evil practice. And neither should anyone try to institute something like infant baptism unless he can prove it from the Bible."

"Have you been rebaptized?" the bailiff asked.

"I had myself baptized by the only baptism I know."

"More than when you were an infant?"

"I was baptized once according to the Scriptures on March 31, 1563," Jan replied.

"Who baptized you? What was his name and where was he from?"

"I did not ask his name. Nor have I seen him since, to my knowledge," Jan responded.

"Where does he live?" the bailiff persisted.

"I don't know."

"You don't know where he was from?" the bailiff asked in disbelief.

"I do not wish to tell you anything about him. I don't want to get anyone in trouble."

"Were there others present when you were baptized?"

"There were," Jan affirmed.

"Who were they?"

"I cannot tell you," Jan replied firmly.

"Where did your baptism take place?" the bailiff asked next.

"In Holland."

"Holland is a big place. Where in Holland?" the bailiff persisted.

"Why should I tell you the place? You will only demand more information, and I do not want to implicate anyone," Jan replied.

After a few more questions in which Jan would not divulge any information, the bailiff switched to a different subject. "How long have you been married? Where did you get married, and who was present?"

"I was married in the Christian church five years ago," Jan answered. To all further questions, he refused to give more information.

"If you don't tell me, we will torture you," the bailiff threatened.

When Jan continued to refuse to give more information, the bailiff muttered, "I wish you were miles from here."

"So do I," Jan agreed.

The jailer was then summoned again and Jan was escorted back to his cell.

Several days later Jan was again taken to the sheriff's hall. This time the bailiff and a priest awaited him. After some animated discussion, the priest asked, "People believe many different things. Is there more than one true faith?"

"No, there is but one true faith," Jan stated firmly.

The priest and Jan continued their discussion, with Jan quoting Scriptures to prove his beliefs.

"You are forever replying with the Holy Scriptures!" the priest finally exclaimed.

"Of course," Jan answered. "What else would I reply with? I have nothing else."

"Yes, but there are things beyond what is written in the Holy Scriptures that we should follow," the priest argued. "Even Paul taught to 'hold the traditions which ye have been taught, whether by word, or our epistle.'[2] So some teachings are passed on simply by

---

[2] 2 Thessalonians 2:15

word and are not written in the Holy Scriptures."

"That may be true," Jan agreed, "but it must always agree with the Scriptures. It cannot require things contrary to them. You must not obscure the real meaning of the Scriptures by your additional teachings—like the teaching that the Communion bread is the actual body and blood of Christ. Is that not what you teach?"

"Yes," the priest replied, "when we have pronounced a blessing on it, it becomes His flesh and blood."

"But I took part in your Communion services before I was converted, and never did the bread feel like flesh in my mouth," Jan asserted. "It always remained bread."

After further debate on different doctrines, Jan was again led back to prison. This time, instead of being put back with the other prisoners, he was placed in a cell by himself. The jailer also took away the Bible the bailiff had permitted him to have when he was first apprehended.

Several weeks passed in which Jan spent rejoicing in God's goodness and fortifying himself in his faith. *How thankful I am for the passages I have memorized! And how good God is to bring them to my mind.*

"Maerten Janss and Jan Hendrickss have confessed to belonging to the evil sect of the Anabaptists and have attended forbidden meetings. They have been rebaptized and continue to persist in their heresy. Therefore they shall be led forth to a scaffold in the marketplace and be burned to death. No one shall speak with them, or they will forfeit their own life and property." The court clerk read the sentence loudly and clearly.

After hearing how their two-year imprisonment would end, the two brethren were led outside to the marketplace. Maerten was tied to the stake first. The executioner seared his tongue to prevent him from talking, but he still spoke out boldly to the crowd that had gathered. "I must testify of the truth. Had I not cared for my salvation, I could have escaped this suffering. But now I have fought a good fight. I have finished my course. I have kept the faith. A crown of righteousness awaits me!" Maerten's voice rang out joyfully over the crowd.

As the flames began to leap around his feet, Maerten prayed aloud, "Lord, be merciful to me. I am not worthy to suffer for your name, but you have made me worthy. Receive my spirit!"

Jan's turn was next. The executioner had gagged him so he couldn't speak, but he still managed to cry out to the crowd, "Now is the time for you to hear the truth!" As his words rang forth, the crowd grew tumultuous.

The rulers ordered Jan to be led back inside until the commotion ceased. When the people became calm again, Jan was again led forth to the scaffold. This time he was securely gagged so no words could be uttered, and the fire soon claimed his earthly life.

Following the executions, the two mangled bodies were taken outside the city to a place called Gallows Hill. Each body was fastened to a stake and left for the birds to eat. But that didn't matter to Maerten and Jan. Their earthly cares and trials were over.

CHAPTER NINETEEN

"I Would Rather Die"

Menen, Belgium—A.D. 1572

Martyrs Mirror pages 962-965

"Good night, my dear," Pierintgen said cheerfully as she tucked the blanket around the frail woman's shoulders. "I must go now. Lord willing, I'll be back in the morning. Sleep well." She stooped and planted a kiss on the wrinkled forehead.

The woman stirred and a feeble hand emerged from under the blanket, reaching for Pierintgen's hand. "Thank you," she whispered as Pierintgen stooped down to hear her words. "What would I do without you? God bless you." The old woman drew the younger woman's hand to her lips briefly.

Pierintgen tucked her in again, patted her on the shoulder, then walked out of the room. Picking up her basket, she stepped outside. The sun was beginning a final descent in the west, casting long shadows. Pausing for a moment, she drank in the beauty of the evening. "It's so peaceful," she murmured to herself.

Pierintgen began to walk toward her home, which was only a few streets away. Halfway there, she met the chief bailiff going the opposite direction. "Good evening," she greeted him pleasantly.

"Halt!" the bailiff ordered. Pierintgen stopped at the command and waited. "Who are you?" he asked. "And where do you live?"

"I live close to here," Pierintgen responded. "I'm on my way home now."

The bailiff's face darkened. "You're coming with me. I just know you're one of those heretics." With those words, he seized her wrists and tied them with a rope. Kicking aside the basket she had dropped, the bailiff led her off toward the prison.

"Lock her up!" he ordered the guard when they arrived.

Pierintgen, stunned by the sudden turn of events, sank onto the narrow ledge that served as a bed and a seat in the cell. Slowly her mind refocused. *I can't believe I'm in prison.*

Two days later, the jailer led her from her cell to appear before the lords for examination. After preliminary questions about who she was and where she lived, the questions intensified. "Do you confess that you are a Christian and that you have attended unlawful assemblies?" one of them asked.

"I am a Christian," Pierintgen confessed freely. "I follow Christ and try to shun evil and do good. Christ tells us in Matthew 18:20 that where two or three are gathered in His name, He is in the midst of them. I could never forsake the assemblies of those who gather in His name, even if it costs me my life."

"Have you been rebaptized?"

"I have been baptized according to the command of Christ. There were those in the early church who had received John's baptism, but when they learned of Christ, they were baptized again in the name of Jesus. One must first believe in Jesus before being baptized. Baptism is the answer of a good conscience toward God."

"Who was present at your baptism?"

"That I cannot tell you," Pierintgen answered firmly.

"We'll make you tell us!" one of the lords threatened.

But no amount of coaxing or threatening could move Pierintgen to disclose any names of those present at her baptism. The lords finally gave up threatening and turned to a different subject. "Do you believe the priests are vicars of Christ and have the power to forgive sin?"

"I cannot agree with that," Pierintgen replied. "Christ was a true Shepherd and laid down His life for His sheep, but the priests would never give their lives for the good of others. Christ is the only true Mediator between God and man. He is the only One who can forgive sins."

"What is your view of the sacrament? Can you confess that Christ's body is indeed in the sacrament once the priest pronounces the blessing on it?"

Pierintgen shook her head. "Mass and all that pertains to it is nothing more than a man-made tradition that God will destroy. Christ left us an example of how to keep His supper in remembrance of Him."

"Surely you believe that every person born into this world is contaminated by the sin of Adam," one lord stated. "So wouldn't it be needful to have that sin washed away as soon as possible, even by baptism when yet an infant?"

"It is the blood of Christ that takes away sin," Pierintgen answered. "Baptism is but a symbol of the cleansing work Christ has already done in the heart."

The lords continued their questioning. "Did not Christ acquire His flesh from His mother Mary?"

"That is not a matter of importance," Pierintgen responded. "The Bible tells us that He was from above and came down from His Father. John tells us the Word became flesh. Christ alone is my Reconciler, my Redeemer, and my Advocate. I need no more knowledge for my salvation."

"Is it right to swear oaths before authorities to establish the truth?" one of the lords asked her next.

Pierintgen responded without hesitation. "Christ answered that question very plainly when He said, 'Swear not at all.'" [1]

"Do you believe that when someone dies, we can do good works that still benefit them?" one lord inquired.

"Certainly not," Pierintgen replied. "'If the tree fall toward the south, or toward the north, in the place where the tree falleth, there it shall be.'[2] Nothing we do can help the dead."

"What shall we do with this woman?" the lords asked one another. "She has an answer for every question. She has been thoroughly deceived into believing false doctrine."

---

[1] Matthew 5:34

[2] Ecclesiastes 11:3

"Bring in the most learned of the priests," one suggested. "Surely they can convince a mere woman."

This suggestion was carried out, and the priests sought to teach Pierintgen the ways of God on their terms. At first they used kind entreaties, but when that failed to move her, they resorted to threats of torture, imprisonment, and even death.

"I would rather die than turn my back on God," Pierintgen declared.

The priests shook their heads. "We cannot reason with her. She must be tortured."

Pierintgen was seized and laid upon the rack. A stick was placed in her mouth and little by little her body was stretched. Her teeth broke into pieces from the pressure of the stick in her mouth, and her arms and legs extended farther and farther.

"Give up your faith and turn back to the state church, then we will release you," the burgomaster urged.

"Tell us the names of others in your church," the priests chimed in. "You don't have to suffer like this. Just give us the information we want."

Pierintgen refused. "As long as God keeps my lips, I shall not betray my brethren. But, oh, that you would release me from this torture!"

"Recant and confess!" the burgomaster said again.

Painfully Pierintgen replied, "I would rather die this temporal death than deny my Lord and forfeit His eternal kingdom."

Finally, seeing they could do nothing to make her confess, they released her from the rack and forced her to walk back to her prison cell.

As Pierintgen lay in her cell, great sadness settled upon her. "God," she prayed, "I fear death. I'm afraid I will weep when they lead me out to die. But I want to be joyful, for I will be coming home to you."

Over the next days, Pierintgen continued to pour out her fears to

God. Finally the day of sentencing came. The bailiff came to lead her to the courtroom. "There is still time to recant," he urged her.

But Pierintgen responded, "He that would obtain the precious prize that is set before us must run without ceasing." Instead of sorrow and sadness, great joy and good cheer filled her heart as she entered the courtroom.

The burgomaster read her sentence aloud, first enumerating her charges. "Because you remain obstinate in your ways, you shall be burned as a heretic." He laid down the report.

On the way to the execution site, Pierintgen called out boldly to the people who were gathering to watch the proceedings. "Go buy a New Testament and read it. Then you will find out why I am sentenced to death."

The executioner turned furiously toward her and raised his hand as if to strike her. "How dare you speak like that! Shut up, you heretic!"

When they arrived at the place of execution, Pierintgen was directed into a small hut that had been erected. There she knelt down and prayed aloud, commending her spirit into the hands of God. As the people watched, the flames leaped around the hut until both it and its occupant were consumed.

But God was not finished. Although Pierintgen had been faithful to the end, God saw fit to bring swift judgment on the one who had sentenced her. Soon afterward, the burgomaster became terribly ill. His flesh decayed so severely that one of his ears dropped off. He died a slow, miserable death.

"I Would Rather Die"

CHAPTER TWENTY

"Here Comes the Wolf"

Workum, Netherlands—A.D. 1574

Martyrs Mirror pages 1005-1007

Hendrick expertly steered his boat through the placid waters of the Zuyder Zee. Off to his left, he could see the outline of the coast of the Netherlands. "It'll be a few more hours before we dock," he said, glancing at his wife. "I'm ready for a good night's rest." Hendrick smothered a yawn and flexed his arms, first one, then the other, as he kept careful control of his boat's course.[1]

---

[1] This story has added details to develop the basic account given in the *Martyrs Mirror*.

"Me too," Trintjen replied, looking up from the pair of socks she was knitting. "It seems long since we left Harderwijk two days ago." She stuck her knitting into the basket by her feet and stood up stiffly. After steadying herself against the smooth motion of the boat, she moved over to stand beside Hendrick. "I still haven't quite gotten used to walking against this constant motion!"

Hendrick grinned. "I remember that first trip after we were married. You preferred sitting in the cabin, because every time you tried to walk around you ended up on the floor! You do a lot better now."

He cast an affectionate smile at his wife. "The trips don't seem half as long as they used to when I was alone. Since you joined me six months ago, these trips haven't been the same. God was so good to bring you into my life."

Trintjen smiled in return. "I never dreamed I would someday spend most of my days on the sea! But then I met you. How different life is now! Yes, God has been good to us." The two continued their reminiscing as the evening passed.

"Hark! What did I hear?" Hendrick's senses kicked into high alert. His eyes searched the water around him and peered into the gathering shadows of the evening.

"Hendrick!" Trintjen's face paled as she clutched his arm. "Look! To the north!"

Hendrick turned his gaze northward and caught sight of a yacht rapidly approaching. "Surely there aren't any pirates around here!" he said, keeping his eyes on the yacht. For a moment he considered trying to pick up speed and outrun the yacht.

"It's no use," he told Trintjen. "We could never outrun them. Their yacht is ten times faster than our boat." His shoulders sagged in defeat. Was his boating career about to end? "If it's pirates…" His voice trailed off. Anyone used to sailing the sea knew the danger of pirates—that anyone caught by them was usually killed or taken prisoner for life. Many, if they had a choice, joined the pirates in their evil lifestyle instead of just wasting away on the boat.

"Halt!" an authoritative voice rang out as the yacht drew up beside them. "In the name of the king of Spain!"

"Oh, no!" Hendrick groaned, loud enough for only Trintjen to hear. "It's the king's men. We are doomed."

As Trintjen drew closer to Hendrick, he laid a protective arm across her shoulders. "Trintjen, my lamb, here comes the wolf. Be brave." His voice became a whisper as the king's men began scrambling aboard their boat. "Try to answer their questions honestly and boldly."

"Where does this craft hail from?" the leader asked roughly.

"From Harderwijk," Hendrick answered politely. He knew Harderwijk was at peace with the king of Spain and thought this might gain him a little favor, for a continual feud festered between Holland and Spain.

The leader deliberated for a moment, then ordered, "You're coming with us." The young couple was forced to board the yacht, and several men commandeered Hendrick's boat.

When the yacht reached the shore the next day near the city of Workum, Hendrick and Trintjen were turned over to the local authorities, who led Hendrick off to prison. Trintjen followed and begged the jailer for permission to speak with her husband. Grudgingly, he finally let her in.

"Hendrick, what shall we do?" Trintjen couldn't hide the anguish in her voice. "How can I secure your release? What can we do?"

Faithful Unto Death

Hendrick spoke with great difficulty. "Trintjen, my dear, seek not my release. It grieves me to tell you, but I have no hope of release. This city is under the control of Spain, and the king of Spain has no mercy on Christians. And I've been told the colonel here is even more brutal than the king. When these men learn that I am a Christian, there will be no hope of letting me go. Only death."

His eyes became wet with tears. "So, my dear, don't seek my release, but rather go to our friends back home and tell them what happened. Perhaps they can secure the release of the boat and then sell it to help pay what we still owe them. They were so kind to help me purchase it." He stared into the distance for a moment.

"Come, let's pray together before we part." The prison cell became hallowed ground as the grieving couple poured out their troubles to God, seeking His comfort.

"Now go, my dear wife. May God speed your journey so you can safely reach home. I'll meet you in heaven." Hendrick tenderly embraced his weeping wife before she departed.

The next morning Hendrick was called before the colonel to be questioned. "Where are you from? Where were you going? Who do you work for?" Question after question flew at Hendrick, and he patiently answered each one.

"Will you swear allegiance to the king of Spain?" the colonel finally asked.

"I will not swear," Hendrick replied firmly. "God commands us in His Word to 'swear not at all.' I give my allegiance to God and Him alone."

The colonel stared at him. "Young man, do you know what you are saying? No one can give allegiance to anyone but the king of Spain!"

"I give my allegiance to God," Hendrick repeated.

The colonel looked around the courtroom. "Men," he said grimly, "we have a man here who is worse than a traitor. He is a heretic!" He spat out the word in disgust.

The court erupted with a roar of anger. "Away with him!" the men shouted. "He is not fit to live!"

The colonel beckoned to the soldiers standing nearby. "Take him!"

The soldiers seized Hendrick and dragged him out of the courtroom. The colonel followed. "I wish we hadn't permitted his wife to leave," he muttered. "I would have liked to see her suffer too."

The men made sport of Hendrick, tormenting him in every way they could think of, but Hendrick bore it all without a word.

"Let's go dunk him in the sea!" one man exclaimed. "He says he liked his life on the sea. Let's see if he still likes it!" He laughed uproariously at his own wit.

"Better yet," said another man as they dragged Hendrick toward the harbor. "He liked his boat. Let's give him one last ride in it!"

"With some tar and some heat," added another.

This suggestion was met with shouts of approval, and one man ran to fetch a supply of tar. After applying tar liberally to Hendrick's boat, they placed him into it and smeared him with tar. They then spread out his arms and bound them to the boat.

The men pushed the boat out into the harbor and set it on fire, watching from a safe distance in their own boat.

"Look! He's moving around!" one of the men shouted.

"His hands are free!" another exclaimed.

"Quick!" the colonel cried in dismay. "Take this sword and kill him before he escapes!"

The soldiers rowed frantically across the water toward the burning boat. They rapidly closed in, and one man plunged his sword through Hendrick. Then they retreated again, allowing the boat to drift to sea as it burned up.

Hendrick's earthly life was over, but along with many others, he had gained the crown of eternal life. He had been faithful—faithful unto death.

Conclusion

And what shall I more say? For the time would fail me to tell of Gideon, and of Barak, and of Samson... {of Antipas and Rufus and Zenobia and Ignatius and Theodosia and Phocus and Eulalia and Narcissus and Julius and Metras and Apollonia and thousands of others...[1]} who through faith subdued kingdoms, wrought righteousness, obtained promises, stopped the mouths of lions, quenched the violence of fire, escaped the edge of the sword, out of weakness were made strong... Others were tortured, not accepting deliverance; that they might obtain a better

---

[1] These are names of people in the *Martyrs Mirror*.

resurrection: and others had trial of cruel mockings and scourgings, yea, moreover of bonds and imprisonment: they were stoned… were tempted, were slain with the sword… being destitute, afflicted, tormented; (of whom the world was not worthy:) they wandered in deserts, and in mountains, and in dens and caves of the earth. Hebrews 11:32-38

We too are called to be faithful. Can we use the freedom we have as an opportunity to grow strong in the Lord and be a witness for Him? "If ye do these things, ye shall never fall," is the promise of 2 Peter 1:10. We will be able to stand firm to the end. We can be faithful, even UNTO DEATH.

- Until now, Christians in America have had an easy life. We know almost nothing of persecution. We have been blessed abundantly to be allowed to live quiet and peaceable lives. But in many other countries, Christians are still being persecuted.

- Now we enjoy freedom to worship God. Will this continue? What if it doesn't? History proves this is not the norm. Are we using our freedom to fortify ourselves so that when persecution comes, we are rooted and grounded in Christ and not easily swayed? Should we become fearful of the "what ifs"?

- There have been some cases in America where Christians have been targeted and treated unfairly because they are Christians. One individual asked an advisor why the officials were being so unreasonable. The answer was, "Your religion." Clearly the officials causing the problems were against Christianity. But as a general rule, Christians are accepted in society.

Over the past few years, we have seen evil exploding in a way we can't fathom. People are openly rebelling against who God created them to be and are even celebrating their perversion. Sin is glorified, and children are taught that good is evil and evil is good. Those who stand for right are being targeted as troublemakers. Some have gone to jail because they did what was right.

Did they expect their stand to take them to jail? Likely not. But they chose to suffer rather than compromise belief. What about you? What about me? Can we, as Daniel of old, bravely continue our lives in the face of those who mock and ridicule us? Even if they try to get us in trouble for staying faithful to God? Could we kneel down and pray just like usual if we knew someone was spying on us to see if we still pray? Or would we slink into some hidden place to pray? Or would we maybe just pray as we go about our work so no one sees what we are doing? It is a challenge we do well to think about.

Every era faces its own forms of persecution. What do we face today? As mentioned earlier, we live in relatively peaceful times. Most of us, if we face any persecution, probably only face mockery at times for our separated way of life. Perhaps our easy life brings questions about persecution. Is persecution God's will? How could God allow the atrocities that happened to His people? Where was God in all those happenings?

All these questions are thought provoking. We cannot answer them exactly. But a few facts stand out. God never forsakes His children, and He sees when His children are persecuted. He knows what has happened in the past and is still happening today in some countries. And He will, in His own time, bring judgment upon evil. Persecution actually causes the church to grow. It also separates the chaff from the wheat, as half-hearted Christianity isn't an option.

*T*o every reader, I challenge you to evaluate your own life. True, Jesus told us not to plan ahead what we will say if we are called to testify for our faith. But will the Holy Spirit bring to our minds things we have never learned? If our Christianity is half-hearted now, how will we be able to testify of our faith when we are called to do so? Is my faith carrying me on? Or am I just coasting along, knowing the right things to say and do without really doing them from the heart?

*H*erein lies the test. Will you pass? All around us are signs that indicate our easy life may not last. While we thank God for our freedom and beseech Him to continue allowing it, we also need to constantly fortify ourselves through His Word. "Fear none of those things which thou shalt suffer…be thou faithful unto death, and I will give thee a crown of life" (Revelation 2:10). May we each be challenged by the faithful examples of those who have gone before us.

A final exhortation from the *Martyrs Mirror:*[2]

My dear friends,

I affectionately greet you as one who is in prison for obedience to the Gospel. God's power is made manifest through my suffering. I rejoice because I know victory through Christ. I have learned that God is a faithful helper in time of need.

Don't be afraid of men, for they cannot harm one hair of the people of God except that He allows it. He will not permit more on us than we can bear. He is able to alleviate pain, as He did for me.

Read the word of God, which will profit you in all things. The Spirit will guide you in understanding. Hearken unto Christ's teachings, and He will be your brother.

I go before you and will wait for you there. No greater joy could we have than to all be together in God's Kingdom!

---

[2] Adapted from a letter by Jan Wouterss to his three youngest sisters, pages 920-921.

About the Author

Marcia Bender grew up in the Finger Lakes region of upstate New York. Throughout her school years, she developed a love for poetry and began writing it. Some of her poems have been published in different periodicals.

Spending time in the classroom as a teacher in west-central Missouri led to practicing story writing skills. And she found she enjoyed that as much as poetry! Over the years, she has had numerous stories published in different periodicals. She often dreamed of someday writing a book.

Following her years in the classroom, she moved to the hills of Kentucky where she worked in the office at Rod and Staff Publishers. Working in a publishing house only deepened her dreams of writing a book. Some of the stories in this book are the direct result of a failed attempt at publishing a book of assorted stories. Even though the initial idea didn't pan out, you now have the results that bloomed from the failure of that seed to sprout.

Marcia now resides in central Wisconsin in a cute little home in the middle of town. She works full time (and more!) managing all aspects of a furniture and home décor store owned by a family from her church. She loves the challenge of running the business and thrives on relating to all the customers she meets. Keeping house, tending the yard, and the necessary life duties keep her beyond busy. But she still squeezes in time to write.

You may write to her at themedleymarket@gmail.com or through CAM Books, P.O. Box 355, Berlin, OH 44610.

About Christian Aid Ministries

Christian Aid Ministries was founded in 1981 as a nonprofit, tax-exempt 501(c)(3) organization. Its primary purpose is to provide a trustworthy and efficient channel for Amish, Mennonite, and other conservative Anabaptist groups and individuals to minister to physical and spiritual needs around the world. This is in response to the command to "Do good unto all men, especially unto them who are of the household of faith" (Galatians 6:10).

CAM supporters provide millions of pounds of food, clothing,

Bibles, medicines, and other aid each year. Supporters' funds also help victims of disasters in the U.S. and abroad, put up Gospel billboards in the U.S., and provide Biblical teaching and self-help resources. CAM's main purposes for providing aid are to help and encourage God's people and bring the Gospel to a lost and dying world.

The Way to God and Peace

We live in a world contaminated by sin. Sin is anything that goes against God's holy standards. When we do not follow the guidelines that God our Creator gave us, we are guilty of sin. Sin separates us from God, the source of life.

Since the time when the first man and woman, Adam and Eve, sinned in the Garden of Eden, sin has been universal. The Bible says that we all have "sinned and come short of the glory of God" (Romans 3:23). It also says that the natural consequence for that sin is eternal death, or punishment in an eternal hell: "Then when lust hath conceived, it bringeth forth sin: and sin, when it is finished, bringeth forth death" (James 1:15).

But we do not have to suffer eternal death in hell. God provided forgiveness for our sins through the death of His only Son, Jesus Christ. Because Jesus was perfect and without sin, He could die in our place. "For God so loved the world that he gave his only begotten Son, that whosoever believeth in him should not perish, but have everlasting life" (John 3:16).

A sacrifice is something given to benefit someone else. It costs the giver greatly. Jesus was God's sacrifice. Jesus' death takes away the penalty of sin for all those who accept this sacrifice and truly repent of their sins. To repent of sins means to be truly sorry for and turn away from the things we have done that have violated God's standards (Acts 2:38; 3:19).

Jesus died, but He did not remain dead. After three days, God's Spirit miraculously raised Him to life again. God's Spirit does something similar in us. When we receive Jesus as our sacrifice and repent of our sins, our hearts are changed. We become spiritually alive! We develop new desires and attitudes (2 Corinthians 5:17). We begin to make choices that please God (1 John 3:9). If we do fail and commit sins, we can ask God for forgiveness. "If we confess our sins, he is faithful and just to forgive us our sins, and to cleanse us from all unrighteousness" (1 John 1:9).

Once our hearts have been changed, we want to continue growing spiritually. We will be happy to let Jesus be the Master of our lives and will want to become more like Him. To do this, we must meditate on God's Word and commune with God in prayer. We will testify to others of this change by being baptized and sharing the good news of God's victory over sin and death. Fellowship with a faithful group of believers will strengthen our walk with God (1 John 1:7).